D1474827

PRAISE FOR NEVER ENOUGH

"Sandra has authentically and poignantly described the practical steps for a full recovery. *Never Enough* will help you embrace radical acceptance of yourself with appropriate guidance in plain language to develop a personalized recovery plan."

–Dr. Peter Selby, Clinician Scientist, Addictions Division Campbell Family Mental Health Research Institute, CAMH

"With her words of love and understanding, Sandra is a beacon of hope that illuminates every situation with optimism. Her incredible insight has earned the admiration of patients, doctors, and academics alike - an inspirational role model for us all! But it's not just her unwavering positivity that stands out; she also seamlessly pairs this outlook with hard scientific evidence to facilitate healing like no one else can. *Never Enough* gives us access to Sandra's inspiring wisdom – definitely something you should not miss!"

–Dr. Sean Wharton, MD, PharmD, FRCP(C), Medical Director Wharton Medical Clinic & Diplomate of the American Board of Obesity Medicine

"Sandra Elia's book *Never Enough* could not come at a better time for society as we begin to confront the long-known science of the impact of ultra-processed 'food like substances' on humans' addiction to food, and its devastating impact on our health and wellbeing. Whether it is from the practical exercises in each chapter, the first-hand accounts of everyday people getting to the other side of food addiction, the 3 pillars to shift from food addiction to food serenity, or numerous other nuggets of wisdom from Sandra's life experiences and professional work, there is something in these pages for anyone at any stage of their journey to find neutrality with food. More importantly, her powerful combination of real talk, science, lived experience, client testimonies, writing style, and a ton of pure love for people, Sandra provides a highly accessible way to help people finally confront the required 'inside work' that they have either avoided, or that has been unavailable to them for years, if not decades."

– Zayna Khayat, Ph.D., Healthcare futurist, Adjunct professor, University of Toronto, Health Sector Strategy at Rotman School of Management

"Sandra Elia offers a spiritual compass for those in need of healing their relationship with food and themselves. She brings clarity to the power of our daily habits and how they influence our body, mind, and spirit. Everything from reframing thought patterns to creating actionable steps is included in her teachings, making them a gift one needs to take advantage of. Truly insightful and inspiring, this book should be read by anyone looking to ignite their healing potential."

–Dr. Sandy Van, MD, CCFP, ABOM Diplomate Obesity Physician Founder, Haven Weight Management

"Sandra has a gift for translating complex concepts into everyday language. *Never Enough* will help you recover, as well as serve as an inspiring call to action."

– Susan Raphael, Mental Health and Addiction Clinician, Substance Abuse Professional (SAP), International Certified Alcohol & Drug Counsellor (ICADC)

Elia, Sandra,
Never enough : three pillars
of food addiction recovery /
2023.
3305357347637
bk   06/25/24

NEVER ENOUGH

THREE PILLARS OF FOOD
ADDICTION RECOVERY

Copyright © 2023 Sandra Elia

All rights reserved. No part of this publication may be reproduced, distributed, or transmitted in any form or by any means without the prior written permission of the publisher, except in the case of brief quotations embodied in critical reviews and certain other noncommercial uses permitted by copyright law.

Disclaimer: This book is not intended as a substitute for the advice of a regulated health professional. The author is not acting as a regulated health professional in this body of work, and this book does not constitute a client-therapist relationship. It is not a replacement for psychology or psychotherapy, and it is recommended that you seek professional support if you feel you need it.

To request permissions, contact the publisher at info@lifetopaper.com.

Hardcover: 978-1-990700-17-0
Paperback: 978-1-990700-18-7
Ebook: 978-1-990700-19-4

First paperback edition March 2023.

Edited by Tabitha Rose, Katrina DeLiberato & Don Loney
Cover photography: Darius Bashar

Printed in the USA.
1 2 3 4 5 6 7 8 9 10

Life to Paper Publishing Inc.
Toronto | Miami

www.lifetopaper.com

LIFE TO PAPER
PUBLISHING

I dedicate this book to the two women in my life who taught me unconditional love…in ways that might surprise you.

To my mom, who taught me **I could love unconditionally**, give, and hope for a better day. My love was unwavering, even though she was too sick to give back.

My daughter taught me to **accept unconditional love**. Despite my shortcomings and the mistakes I've made, her love for me is unwavering. Sofia, you are the greatest blessing in my life, and I will spend all my days being grateful for you.

"Be kind, gentle, and loving to yourself.
Why?
We all flourish in this kind of environment."

SANDRA ELIA

CONTENTS

FOREWORD

Never Enough: Three Pillars of Food Addiction Recovery tackles one of society's best kept secrets—food addiction. It is the most prevalent, the most shameful, and the deadliest force driving the current obesity and diabetes epidemic in our Western world. This book is an attempt to grapple with and respond to this terrible condition, written by a clinician who is herself in long-term recovery from food addiction. She knows her stuff from the inside out.

I met Sandra Elia seven years ago when she interviewed me about food addiction for a university radio show. She was thrilled to meet me, a physician, who was also trying to spread awareness about addiction to disordered eating. Here was another person who recognized that some trigger foods, such as sugar and flour, cause an overwhelming biological desire to compulsively overeat. She understood this painful reality intimately because she had been plagued by compulsive overeating her entire life and had suffered many years with the resulting obesity.

That day, Sandra wanted to broadcast her solution: She had discovered that whenever she treated her compulsive overeating as an addiction instead of as a moral failing, a lack of willpower, or an unwillingness to change, she was able to manage her eating and lose her unhealthy weight. With this radical perspective, she discovered her obsession with food and her weight, the most agonizing issue of her life, could finally be tamed, not just for the short term, but forever.

Sandra was eager to share this news that had so dramatically improved her life. However, she was discouraged to find that while people were eager to hear another remedy for weight-loss, they were not interested in her solution, namely cutting out sugar and flour. Family and friends, fellow sufferers, even medical clinicians who treated eating disorders and obesity were dismissive and skeptical. They claimed that her recommendations were absurd because "food cannot be addictive—we all have to eat!" and "It is impossible to never eat sugar again!" This disbelief persisted despite Sandra's obvious success. Could they not see the transformation in her? Did they not recognize in Sandra immense relief from her misery, substantial weight-loss, and an ability to finally thrive as the person she had always wanted to be?

Sandra was not dissuaded. As soon as I met her, I realized that she enjoys competitive speaking. She somehow inspires dubious, reluctant audiences to action. She has also mined her inner strengths through a daily meditative practice that has enabled her to transform her food sobriety into a personal and professional platform of food serenity. She has honed her skill with dogged perseverance.

From broadcasting her university radio program, to joining Obesity Canada (a clever way to push the message of food addiction to the bariatric clinicians treating obesity, who still primarily treat using medications and surgery, experiencing only moderate success), to taking formal INFACT training in food addiction, to helping us at Renascent Treatment Center create an inpatient food addiction program. She did what she needed to do to arm herself against a world of skeptics. Then Sandra expanded her educational vision to include helping individuals. Over the last six years, she has developed virtual, weekly, and monthly programs to help people recover from food addiction. She is committed to making this treatment accessible to as many people as possible.

Never Enough captures all aspects of Sandra's strengths, vision, and achievements. This book is a three-part endeavor: 1) a revealing memoir of a bottom-of-the-barrel food addict who rises to recovery, 2) a Food Addiction Handbook chock full of explanations, tools, and techniques designed to help the desperate food addict recover, and 3) a powerful call to action that combines the self-help coaching tools and spiritual practices necessary to make the major life changes required for any individual to successfully heal from their food addiction. This book is ideal for someone completing Elia's various food addiction programs or anyone wanting a solid program to battle food addiction. It's packed with motivation, hope, and practical advice.

Bottom line, Never Enough is Sandra's manifesto, a vision statement and guide written by one of the food addiction leaders in the field. As more people acknowledge the manipulations of the food industry, worry about sugar's effects on the brain and body, and suffer the illnesses caused by a lifetime of eating processed foods, a gradual awakening will occur. We need to change our diets—or at the very least, quit sugar and flour. Sandra's book gives us the why's and how-to's to finally do this. And she conveys them with kindness and compassion—key ingredients to make healing and lasting recovery possible for us as individuals and as a society.

Vera Tarman, MD, ABAM
Author of Food Junkies: Recovery from Food Addiction

NEVER ENOUGH

THREE PILLARS OF FOOD
ADDICTION RECOVERY

SANDRA ELIA

DEAREST ONE,

Welcome, welcome…welcome home. My heart's desire is that you return to the home that exists inside of you. The Real You. First, I invite you to let go of the baggage you're carrying. The heavy bags of shame, regret, and guilt. You cannot carry this heavy load on the path of recovery. I'll walk alongside you through the pages of this book. This is a warm, loving, and accepting place where I see you, and I believe the very best about you.

There is nothing you have done to your body with food that I haven't done myself. There's nothing in your past or present that cannot be healed. You hold the key to the magnificence inside of you. We were all born with the spark of the Divine. This calm, confident, wise spark still lives in you today. As food addicts, we often lose our connection to the Divine within and the Divine outside of ourselves. The little voice inside of you begging you to stop "using" food, the knowledge that this is not the life you were intended to live, the whisper of truth that you are misaligned with your purpose and worth—the only way to drown out this voice is to "use" food to obliviate these painful feelings. This numbing comes with the heavy price of blocking out all feelings, including happiness, worthiness, and joy.

The first step on this path is total acceptance and unconditional love for yourself. Why? Because self-hatred and self-condemnation will drain you of every ounce of motivation and energy you have. Love is always energizing. And how much energy will you need for this journey? Every ounce you can summon. But don't let that deter you. I walk this path each and every day, and I will show you the way.

I want you to know that there's nothing wrong with you. You were born a perfect being, and then stuff happened to you. Horrible, frightening, sad things happened to you. Food comforted you through these dark times. This comfort turned into an addiction, and this addiction is now unmanageable.

So, you lost your way, forgot your magnificence. Take a leap of faith with me and believe a calm, confident, wise spark still lives in you. Your only job is to remember and connect with the Divine that already accepts and unconditionally loves you as you are. Come with me to find the Real You.

Much love,
Sandra

YOU ARE LOVED.
YOU ARE WORTHY.
YOU ARE ENOUGH.

My life's work and sincere desire is to guide those struggling with food addiction to a place where they can achieve food serenity. I know first-hand the struggles of compulsive eating and how this addiction can take over a life. I know the pain, the constant pain. One client stands out in my mind as a perfect example of how the three pillars can transform your life for good.

Meet Jannet

My story is all too familiar. I remember always being hungry as a child. No matter how much I ate, it was never enough. As a teenager, I felt bad about myself, experienced cruel teasing from classmates for being "fat," and thought I had weak self-control. For years, I felt trapped in a cycle of compulsive eating and food addiction, never quite understanding why I couldn't kick the habit no matter how painful it was or how hard I tried.

On September 20, 2017, I joined Sandra's Food Addiction Recovery Program in which she shared knowledge gained from her own personal journey of self-empowerment in pursuit of freedom from food addiction. We discussed the reality that food addiction can be just as debilitating as any other addiction and that the road to recovery is often just as long and difficult. We also talked about how it is possible to overcome compulsive eating and build a healthy relationship with food. Sandra shared a powerful video from a CBC documentary on the sugar industry and provided a handout that listed foods known to trigger cravings—as well as addictions—to those foods. I was surprised to see certain ingredients on the list that I never would have thought were triggers to food addiction. Many of these foods were traditionally used in meals prepared by my British family, such as flour, cheese, cream, and other fatty ingredients. Once I learned this first tool and was aware of which foods were potential triggers for addiction, I became better equipped to make choices that would support me in my recovery as I planned and prepared more nourishing and satisfying meals.

I had tried every fad diet on the market, but nothing seemed to work long-term. I would lose a few pounds only to gain them back—and then some. I began to feel hopeless, as if I were destined to be overweight forever. But once I learned about Sandra's approach, I became more confident that achieving and sustaining a healthy weight was possible. I was better able to abstain from trigger foods, such as processed and refined foods—many of which are high in sugar. I was hesitant at first, thinking this might be another fad diet promising rapid, lasting weight-loss but leaving you feeling worse than when you started.

But this program worked—and continues to work!

I gained a sense of ownership over my life's journey. No one would condemn me for failing to achieve my goal weight if I didn't follow the rules to the letter. The power to succeed in my weight-loss journey now rested fully in my hands rather than in those of some flawed program that set me up to fail by including sugar and refined foods in its meal plans or pre-packaged meal offerings. As part of the Food Addiction Recovery Program, I documented where my vulnerabilities lied with the foods I craved most. It was empowering for me to acknowledge the connection between those foods and my self-destructive cravings.

My biggest "aha!" moment came when I learned more about the food industry's deceptive practices. In particular, when it came to the way this industry has exploited—and continues to exploit—emerging science to create chemically-engineered substances designed to make certain foods more addictive. The food I had consumed all my life was engineered by an industry more interested in profits than public health, from the Pablum I was fed as a baby to the countless freezer-to-table meals I ate from childhood well into adulthood. It was a lightbulb moment for me, realizing that my prior addictions to tobacco and alcohol were also tied to the sugar content that intensified in the refining process and made them more addictive. These revelations helped me recover from food addiction and compulsive eating by showing me that I was not alone and that these constant feelings of hunger were not my fault but were instead engineered by the food industry.

Once I understood the truth about sugar and its effect on the brain, I knew where I had to focus my efforts to break free from food addiction and stay on the road to recovery. Knowledge is power when it comes to food addiction, and there is hope for those struggling to escape the grip of this disease.

One of the reasons food addiction is so difficult to overcome is because our brains are designed to scan the surrounding environment at all times, looking for food. Finding and consuming calorie-dense and sugary foods is how our ancestors survived. This drive remains within us today—only now, the food in our environment is toxic. This means we must constantly be on guard against our impulses and cravings.

Even though it sounds incurable, there is hope for recovery. One of the critical tools that can help us achieve food serenity is listing the physical, mental, and emotional symptoms of sugar withdrawal. Seeing the wide range of potential symptoms can be eye-opening, helping us understand the importance of abstaining from sugar and processed foods. Additionally, knowing that some of these symptoms may persist for weeks or even months can help us persevere through the early stages of recovery. Armed with time and knowledge, I began to overcome my cravings and found that compulsive eating was no longer a problem. I had reclaimed my life!

It is well-known that food and emotions are interconnected. What I learned from applying the program every day is how feelings and "comfort foods" play off each other in a never-ending cycle. Although I now avoid processed foods and sugars, I still find myself craving certain foods from time to time. However, having learned the connection between emotional triggers and particular foods, I feel empowered to recognize when an emotionally triggering experience disguises itself as a craving. I understand that I should spend time with that feeling to understand its source rather than suppress it with food.

I also learned that even when I feel emotionally content and happy, my body can still respond to outside food stimuli tied to a positive memory. A good example of this is when I smell freshly baked bread. It reminds me of her mother's baking. I have a positive emotional connection with that particular food, so I feel emotionally compelled to bake (and eat) sourdough bread. The experience makes me feel connected to my deceased mother.

For me, it was another "aha!" moment. Recognizing an emotion, whether positive or negative, or a physical symptom, such as fatigue, can and often does trigger a craving for particular foods. Being aware of this fact gave me the power to choose how to respond. That in itself was self-empowering and helped me re-establish my emotional equilibrium while staying healthy and active. Recovery from food addiction is a lifelong journey, but now, each day that I am able to make choices rooted in self-love and compassion, I feel I have achieved what can only be described as food serenity.

The next critical tool for success Sandra shared with me was to stop weighing myself. It is more important to see and feel the real progress being made over time than it is to focus on an arbitrary number on your scale. Weight can fluctuate widely from day to day for a variety of reasons often unrelated to food intake. Seeing that number on the scale fluctuate can affect your emotions, triggering "comfort eating," and potentially derailing your recovery from food addiction. Instead, focusing on the true progress that is being made helps keep people in recovery, where they remain motivated and continue achieving their goals.

For instance, I documented my weight once a month and noted that there was a six-month period where my weight-loss stagnated even though there was no change in my daily healthy eating practice. I initially felt concerned and conflicted as to whether I had plateaued or the program no longer worked, but I remembered Sandra's advice: "Do not take your weight because it can affect you emotionally." I decided to follow this guidance and made a pact with myself that regardless of the number I read on the scale, whether it was higher, lower, or unchanged, I would stay focused on my life-affirming goal of health, vitality, and freedom from food cravings—the foundation of Sandra's Food Addiction Recovery Program.

I regularly update Sandra on my progress. Here is my latest correspondence:

Wanted to share a milestone in my journey of carb sobriety. Today marks the thirtieth day of the fourth month in my fifth year since beginning your program. I only weigh myself once every thirty days, so today I checked the number on the scale against a BMI chart for a healthy weight-to-height ratio. I am right in the middle of a healthy BMI and have been at this weight for several months. Since coming to your first class and following your program, my body has slowly but progressively released eighty-five pounds. I turn sixty-five next week, and I cannot think of a better gift to myself than that of good health and freedom from the pain and other health- and mobility-related issues that plagued me for so many decades before learning the skills and fortitude to break my addiction to carbs. I landed a great new job about ten months ago and again, due to a healthy diet and moderate aerobic exercise, I also feel cognitively way younger than others on the bell-curve. Sandra, I feel "at peace" with food. I feel food is "at peace" with me. I also feel empowered to live my life as I wish to live it: active, youthful, engaged, and happy.

Jannet's story is a powerful example of: (a) the strength that comes from knowing the underlying factors that can and often do lead to food addiction and compulsive overeating, and (b) the empowerment we experience when equipped with the tools to support our commitment to overcoming food addiction.

For many people struggling with compulsive eating, the goal of recovery can seem out of reach. But as Jannet's story demonstrates, significant change is possible when practitioners persevere through the Food Addiction Recovery Program and remain open to self-discovery. Jannet's story also highlights the importance of staying focused on the purpose underlying one's healthy eating goals, even when progress seems slow or elusive. It's easy to get discouraged when we don't see the results we want right away. But, like Jannet, trust in the process and remember that the program's core purpose is to provide the skills and supports necessary to live a life free from food addiction. Even when you face challenging days and events, stay the course. Achieving wellbeing is not a race to an arbitrary finish line; it is a continual, life-affirming meditation. Thanks to her own courage and determination, Jannet is living proof that food addiction doesn't have to control your life.

Lasting change is possible. There will be times when you don't just FEEL free from your addiction to trigger foods. You WILL BE free. And with this freedom, you will experience life from an entirely different perspective, one that opens you up to engage it fully and live it however best supports your long-term health, vitality, and wellbeing.

When There Was "Never Enough" for Me

I understand Jannet's struggle. I know what "never enough" feels like. Never enough diets. Never enough food to fully numb the pain. Never enough love. I was never enough. I spent years obsessing over food, dieting, and my weight. I was never satisfied with myself, and I was always chasing after an impossible standard. But what I eventually realized was that the problem wasn't with me—it was with the way I lived my life. I was basing my worth on something completely out of my control.

Let me take you back to 2001, the time when "never enough" ruled my life. I was twenty-nine years old and weighed 262 pounds, and if you know me, you know I am all of five feet, two inches tall. It was a dark, sad, rock-bottom place in my life.

There was never enough food to numb the pain. I was compulsively overeating, usually three to five times a week. I used food as my primary source of strength and comfort. It eventually became my all-mighty drug.

Even though I used tremendous amounts of food to "numb out," my drug left me empty. I felt nothing but the pain of that emptiness. I felt like an outcast, as though I had no right to exist in this world that values beauty so highly.

There were never enough diets. I was unhappy with my physical appearance for many years, and I tried every fad diet out there. I would lose weight, but then I would gain it all back again—plus more. I felt like a failure. I didn't understand why I could not stick to a diet. I felt like something was wrong with me. *Why couldn't I be like everyone else and lose the weight and keep it off?* I became very critical of myself and felt trapped by the burden of my low self-esteem. I hinged my self-worth on my physical appearance and the number on the scale.

Being myself was never enough.

My size always measured my worth. The bigger my size, the less I was worth. The truth was that my weight was merely a manifestation of the life I lived, a life completely out of control.

I was twenty-nine years old, and I was ready to check out. I had been through a lot in a short amount of time. I was clinically depressed and in a bad marriage. I was taking care of my mom, who was living with bipolar disorder and obesity, without any boundaries in place. I ended up taking an extended sick leave from work. Life was something I could not master, and addiction was running the show. I wanted to understand why and where I was broken. And so, I began to ask myself a series of questions:

- Was I in a relationship that nurtured my spirit and enhanced my life? *Not many would describe my marriage this way.*
- Was I in a career that inspired me? *I was at a point where I could not work. Just brushing my teeth and combing my hair was almost too much for me to handle.*
- Had I set the necessary boundaries to enjoy a healthy family life? *Taking care of my mentally-ill mom was devastating for my family. At the time, I struggled to imagine how I could have put boundaries in place to manage my own health. It was possible. I just hadn't realized it yet.*
- What were the thoughts that occupied my mind, and were they energizing? *My mind was filled with thoughts of self-hatred, disgust, and judgment, and they drained me of every ounce of energy and motivation I had.*
- What connection did I have to my spirit? *I was completely disconnected from my spirit. I had severed ties. That was the only way I could live in such dysfunction.*

When any of these areas of my life caused me pain—and all of them did—food became my coping mechanism. To this day, when I am not constructively dealing with my life, I am in pain, and when I am in pain, I am in jeopardy of using food.

In this book, I will break down every excuse you can conjure for why you are never enough. I will show you that it is time for you to step into your power and claim the life you were meant to live. It is your time to stop believing the lies we (and others) tell ourselves—that we are not good enough, that we are powerless, and that food is the only thing that can make us feel better. But it doesn't have to be this way. Healing is possible, and I will show you how to take back control of your life. Food addiction and compulsive eating don't have to rule your life. You can be free from their grip. It's time to step into your power and claim the life you were meant to live.

Food serenity is about finding peace and neutrality with food. This means eliminating your trigger foods, developing spirituality and mindfulness, and belonging to a support network.

Eliminating your trigger foods is the FIRST PILLAR of achieving food serenity. Trigger foods are those that we are compulsively drawn to eat, even when we're not hungry. They trigger cravings and lead to overeating. Common trigger foods include refined sugar, refined carbs, ultra-processed food, and food high in saturated fat.

The SECOND PILLAR of food serenity is developing spirituality and mindfulness. Addictive eating is often mindless eating. One of the remedies is mindfulness. If you've struggled with your weight or eating for years, maybe even decades, it can chip away at your self-esteem. Spirituality is a remembering of your worth and connecting to the power that lies within you. Spirituality can be practiced through meditation, prayer, journaling, or nature walks.

The THIRD PILLAR is belonging to a support network. This could be a group of friends or family who support your healing, a therapist or a coach, a sponsor, or an online community. These people can provide encouragement and accountability as you work towards food serenity.

Finally, it's important to have an internal environment that is kind, gentle, and nurturing. Why? Because we flourish in this kind of environment.

Under the Willow Tree

Nature is my happy place. I love meditating in the woods under a particular willow tree. My mom taught me to appreciate and love the shade of a willow tree on a warm summer day. I have a favorite spot in Markham, Ontario, a short walk from where I used to live.

I find my spot beneath the long, low-hanging branches and look over the body of water in front of me, so peaceful and calming. In those moments, I feel so connected to all of life. I feel the earth underneath me. It grounds me and makes me feel safe and protected. I am surrounded by lush greenery and hear a choir of birds chirping happily. I am so grateful for this beautiful earth that I get to live on. It is such a gift.

On this day, I'm struggling and I'm desperate not to be a food addict. From a deep sorrow, I cry out to God: *I don't want to be a food addict!*

Out of nowhere, I hear, "You aren't a food addict…and you never were." It's astounding, as if the earth shakes beneath me.

I'm not sure if the voice is real, or if I am just imagining it. But then the voice speaks again: "You are loved. You are worthy. You are enough." I know now that it's real. It is God. She is speaking to me.

That day changed everything for me. I had struggled with food addiction for many years. On that day, I learned that my identity had nothing to do with being a food addict. I am so much more than that. I am a devoted mother, a caring teacher, and a woman of faith. Food addiction does not define me. It is just the label for an affliction I have—like a diagnosis—and it helps me understand that I need treatment. I need to lead my life a certain way to be well. And I believe God wanted me to know that. She loves me and sees beyond my struggle with food.

The God that created the beautiful green and blue planet we call Earth also created me and you. This world contains the same beauty, imperfections, and resilience that live inside of me and you. And that knowledge has helped me find freedom from food addiction.

For so long, I defined myself as a food addict. It was like a label that I couldn't shake no matter how hard I tried. And it wasn't just me; it was how others saw me too. And it seemed like there was this constant pressure to prove that I was cured. But the truth I was gifted under the willow tree is that healing is possible, even if it feels as if it's beyond our wildest expectations. Healing is about being whole, not about being perfect. It occurs through spirituality, mindfulness, and an understanding that you are not now, and never have been, a food addict. It's just an affliction you have that needs treatment.

I am a daughter, a sister, and—my greatest joy—a mother. I am someone who loves to laugh and have fun. I am someone who is capable of making positive change in the world. And most importantly, I am someone who is loved by God. It took me a long time to realize that my worth doesn't come from what others think of me—it comes through the loving eyes of God. When I finally understood that, it was like a weight had been lifted off my shoulders. I no longer had to prove anything to anyone. I could just be myself. And that is the best feeling in the world.

If you are like I once was, I can say with all certainty that there is nothing wrong with you. And there never was. You just have some work to do: Eliminate trigger foods, develop spirituality and mindfulness, and find a support network. These THREE PILLARS will work to undo the stories (and lies) you tell yourself, the beliefs instilled in you by others, and the misguided conviction that you are never enough.

Always look at yourself, the world, and the people around you through the eyes of love. It is always within you.

If you want to see the world through the eyes of love, it has to start with you. You have to learn to love yourself first. Only then can you start to see the good in the world and the people around you. It is not always easy to do this. The world can be a harsh place, and life can be difficult. But if you can find a way to look at yourself and the world through the eyes of love, it will make all the difference. You will see the beauty in life and in people, even when they are at their worst. You will find compassion for yourself and others. And you can build a more loving world for everyone.

You Are Enough

You are enough just as you are. You don't need to change a thing. All the criticisms you've internalized—they're not true. They're lies that you've believed about yourself, and it's time to let them go. It's time to see yourself through loving, kind eyes, to see yourself as someone worthy of love and respect—someone who is whole and complete just as you are today. It's time to honor your body, mind, and soul, to treat yourself with kindness, compassion, and care. It's time to undo all the damage done and to start fresh. Time to forgive yourself for all the times you've been hard on yourself. Time to love yourself unconditionally and completely. Because you deserve it. And because it's time for you to finally see the truth—that there is nothing wrong with you, and there never was.

You are not your food addiction. You are not your compulsive eating. You are not your past failures or current struggles. You are SO MUCH MORE than that.

It's time to see yourself through loving, wise, compassionate eyes. It's time to see yourself as the beautiful, worthy person you are.

Your food addiction does not define you. Your compulsive eating does not define you. Your healing defines you. Your strength defines you. Your resilience defines you. Your courage defines you.

If your relationship with yourself is the most important relationship in your life, how much time, energy, and consideration are you going to put into it?

The most important relationship in your life is the one you have with yourself. This is the relationship that shapes how you see the world and interact with others. If you're not taking care of yourself, it's difficult to have healthy relationships with others. That's why it's so important to be mindful of your self-care routine. Are you eating food that makes you feel good? Are you getting enough sleep? Are you taking time for yourself every day? If not, now is the time to start. Put yourself first, and the rest will fall into place.

You are not alone. We can do this together.

CHAPTER ONE

AM I A FOOD ADDICT?

Tape Reel: Ruled By the Scale, SEPTEMBER 2001

The tape reel running in my head starts before my eyes even open in the morning: It's a new day, and I fucking hate my life. Waking up, I wonder where I am at first. I can see the living room floor illuminated by the sun streaming through the sliding glass door… I realize I am on the couch—again. I can no longer sleep on a flat bed because my body is too heavy. It aches. And so I sleep in the living room on the loveseat so that I can prop up my legs and save my lower back from hurting as much.

To begin with, I have a food hangover, and I don't know how I will make it through the morning. I don't even want to make it through the morning. I don't want to face my day, myself, or the mirror. I don't want to see my husband. I just want to be alone, alone and comforted by my drug of choice—ultra-processed foods. My drug is killing me.

Later that morning, I weigh myself, and my thoughts begin to distort. I have lost two pounds since last week. But somehow that is not good enough. I have fallen short of the bargain I struck with myself to lose the 100 pounds I'd gained in the last eighteen months. I hate my body, I hate the way I eat, and I hate myself. I have decided that I want to lose one pound a day. If I can't do that, I am a failure.

*I want to find the strength to stop weighing myself. Shouldn't it be enough that I am caring for myself regardless of what I weigh? I want to measure my success by how I treat myself and whether I am overcoming my compulsion to overeat. A successful day should mean I have nourished myself, gotten my body moving, expressed kind words of encouragement for myself, participated in life, and used my time wisely—**NOT THAT I HAD DEFIED THE LAWS OF PHYSICS TO LOSE A POUND.***

I want to give up. If only I could find a way to love myself today and feel worthy, then tomorrow could be better.

I am struggling with the thought of starting another diet. I want a program to tell me what to do and validate my eating. I am scared that I can't do it on my own—that I am not capable of understanding what is best for my body. I can't trust my own thinking when it comes to eating. This idea of eating to nourish my body is foreign to me. If I am not depriving myself, then I can't be succeeding.

This was me at rock bottom, the darkest point in my life. I was twenty-nine and out of control, detached from my body, my feelings, and my passions. I was merely going through the motions of each day, seeing only what was directly in front of me, knowing only the task at hand. I did not have the strength to plan, dream, or focus my strength on anything but surviving.

Using food as my only source of strength and comfort made it my drug of choice—and it was a powerful one. But this drug ultimately left me empty. I lived with the fact that I was more than 100 pounds overweight, I was perpetually uncomfortable, and I felt undesirable. My entire body ached, and I could no longer move freely. I isolated myself from friends, activities, and the world. I felt like an outcast, as though I had no right to play a part in this world that values beauty so highly. My worth is measured by my size—the bigger I was, the less I am worth to myself.

To make matters worse, I projected these feelings onto others, thus fulfilling my fears and confirming my distortions. Food was running my life. It was unmanageable. *I* was unmanageable.

When I compulsively overate, I forgot about everything. And for those precious few moments of eating, the voices in my head were silent. But once I finished, I felt the pain and suffering all over again—except worse.

I hated myself. I hated everyone around me. I hated the voices in my head, and they hated me even more. My weight was costing me my marriage, jobs, friendships, and opportunities. My weight had become the reason I was NOT capable of living the life I wanted.

I found myself looking for a way to end the pain.

At that point, my life could have been summed up in three words: Desperate. Hopeless. Decimated.

I felt like I had no choice but to either end everything or change everything.

I chose to change. I knew there was no way to avoid confronting the events in the past that became the source of my present pain. There was nowhere to run and no place to hide anymore if I wanted to heal.

Tape Reel: Discovering My Coping Mechanism, NOVEMBER 1977

I am a picky eater. I am very little and thin. Not eating means my mom will show concern, and I enjoy that. Tonight, my mother and my older sister are fighting in the TV room in our basement. I am terrified and desperate for it to stop. I run to the kitchen, grab some cheese and bread, sit at my mom's feet, and start eating in front of her to please her. The fighting stops, and my mother does something I don't remember her doing before. She praises me. It feels so good to know that I changed things. For one moment, I feel like I have control over the chaos of my environment.

But then the fighting starts again. This time, it wakes my father. My other sister runs down the steps, crying. Ma hurriedly locks herself in the bathroom. Then I hear Pa's heavy footsteps charging down the stairs toward the basement, and as he blows by me, I see that he has his belt in his hand. I freeze. My brain can't comprehend what's happening. In a flash, I run to my brother, grip onto his arm, and beg him to make it stop.

The rest of the night is pretty foggy for me. Even at four years old, I somehow feel like our life as a family will never be the same again. I will never trust my father again or feel comfortable in his presence. It is the end of my innocence, the end of sanctity in our home. For a brief moment, food had calmed the storm. Food had power. I had found a coping mechanism, albeit a very destructive one. The belief was set—food could make things better.

Food: A Powerful Drug

Food is one of our most basic needs, but for some people, certain foods trigger overwhelming "feel-good brain chemicals" that overtake their brain's reward pathway. And they can't stop eating. Literally.

In the same way that someone who smokes craves a cigarette or a person who lives with alcoholism can't stop after one drink, there are some folks who simply can't stop eating after they take that first bite. Their brain is hijacked. Chemicals start racing, and the addictive cycle has begun. We call this food addiction. The Food Addiction Institute (foodaddictioninstitute.org) offers a clinical definition:

> Food addiction is a disease which causes loss of control over the ability to stop eating certain foods. Scientifically, food addiction is a cluster of chemical dependencies on specific foods or food in general; after the ingestion of high-palatable foods such as sugar, excess fat and/or salt, the brains of some people develop a physical craving for these foods. Over time, the progressive eating of these foods distorts their thinking and leads to negative consequences, which they do not want but cannot stop.

If someone eats when they really do not want to, if they persistently eat more food than their body needs, or if they eat in a way that they know is not good for them, they may be a food addict. There are a number of tests and questionnaires for assessing food addiction (like the Yale Food Addiction Scale, YFAS).

Food addiction is similar to drug and alcohol addiction. Addiction means the body has become chemically dependent on one or more substances and needs these substances to cope with life. So when we talk about a specific food potentially becoming a substance of abuse, we mean that the body has become dependent on a particular food or eating behavior. The most common addictive foods are foods high in refined sugar, refined flour, fat, salt, or some combination of these. The most common addictive eating behaviors are binging, purging, and volume eating.

Food addiction is a chronic and progressive disease characterized by seeking addictive foods or food behaviors, engaging them compulsively, and having a great deal of difficulty controlling these urges despite their harmful consequences.

When we initially consumed these same foods as children, we might have had the choice of when and how much to eat them. But repeated use can lead to brain changes that trick the mind, challenge an addicted person's ability to choose, and interfere with their ability to resist consuming these foods or engaging in unwanted, harmful eating behaviors. These brain changes are persistent. This is why food addiction can be complicated to treat. People often go on a "diet" for a while and think they're fine: "See I can quit eating _____(fill in the blank). I'm fine. I'm not an addict." However, once someone is addicted, "dieting" for a period of time is rarely a successful long-term solution.

How do you know if you are a food addict? Ask yourself the following questions, and keep track of how many times you answer yes:

1. Have I ever wanted to stop eating and found I just can't?
2. Do I think about food or my weight constantly?
3. Do I find myself attempting one diet or food plan after another with no lasting success?
4. Do I binge eat and then counteract it through vomiting, exercise, laxatives, or other forms of purging?
5. Do I eat differently in private than I do in front of other people?
6. Has a doctor or family member ever approached me with concerns about my eating habits or weight?
7. Do I eat large quantities of food at one time (binge)?
8. Is my weight problem due to my "nibbling" all day long?
9. Do I eat to escape from my feelings?

10. Do I eat when I'm not hungry?
11. Have I ever discarded food only to retrieve and eat it later?
12. Do I eat in secret?
13. Do I fast or severely restrict my food intake?
14. Have I ever stolen other people's food?
15. Have I ever hidden food to make sure I have "enough"?
16. Do I feel driven to exercise excessively to control my weight?
17. Do I obsessively calculate the calories I've burned against the calories I've eaten?
18. Do I frequently feel guilty or ashamed about what I've eaten?
19. Am I waiting for my life to begin "when I lose the weight"?
20. Do I feel hopeless about my relationship with food?[1]

If you answer yes to three or more of these questions, this book is for you. Know that you are not alone.

You'll hear me say this often: **My weight is none of my business.**

My business is to eat whole foods and move my body. The real work is to love and appreciate the body I have today. My weight is God's business.

Is It Time to Break Up with Your Scale?

"Am I thin enough? Am I enough? Do I need to lose weight?"

The answers to these questions were my biggest and deepest fears. And if you've ever asked yourself these questions, I see you. Because I *am* you. These fears cycled through my head every day, making my decisions for me when it came to my weight, what I ate, and what I did about it. I lost control over my eating behavior, and this led me to spend excessive time focused on food, compulsively overeating and recuperating from food hangovers.

Food addiction robbed me of my life. It robbed me of my mother, my childhood, my emotional growth and maturity, and even my romantic relationships. I found solace in food. It soothed me. It soothed the heartache and sense of feeling unloved, unseen, and unheard. This book is not about punishing yourself with strict and extreme diets. Instead, it's about affirming your life. As I share how I overcame my food addiction and learned to live a life bursting with

---

[1] "Am I A Food Addict", Food Addicts in Recovery Anonymous, 2022, https://www.foodaddicts.org/am-i-a-food-addict?gclid=Cj0KCQiA37KbBhDgARIsAIzce14qSiX8r5wcfvIOF92HakHasF6NC9zQ2VOkNo_y_dLZixOvj6QhegaAkVXEALw_wcB

self-love and self-care, I hope you will realize the same is possible for you. This book is about changing your perception of who you are to the point where, once you see the truth, you will never *unsee* it.

If you are truly doing your best by eating the freshest whole foods available, moving your body, and practicing self-love every day, why would you need to know your weight?

I want you to consider whether your relationship with the scale is healthy or abusive. Is it based solely on your physical body? Does the scale consider who you are as a person, what you've accomplished, and how you contribute to the world? Do you give the scale the power to ruin your day? To dictate if you've been good or bad? To determine whether you should eat or not? Is your prize the number on the scale?

Starting today, I challenge you to stop letting the number on the scale define you. Your prize shouldn't be how much you weigh but how great you feel!

In my food serenity journey, I have learned to love and appreciate my body, and consequently, I've attracted people who love and appreciate me and my body. My body isn't for everyone—but once it was right for me, that was all that mattered.

My body isn't perfect, but I am perfectly in love with it. This is possible for you too, but it all begins with that mental shift towards acceptance and unconditional love. Once you achieve this, you'll see yourself and the world around you through a whole new, bright light, one that will guide your journey to becoming the healthiest you can be and living a fulfilling life.

Achieving Peace with Yourself Is Achieving Peace with Food

Growing up plagued by fear, I often turned to food for emotional support, safety, and peace. As a child, each year when I blew out the candles on my birthday cake, my only wish was for peace. I was desperate for a stable home, and food seemed to be my only source of comfort and escape. I witnessed my mother's spiral into food addiction, and I hoped I would never follow in her footsteps.

It took time to recover from my own food addiction, and it took strength and resilience to keep going, but I finally arrived at a place where I feel at peace with myself. I learned that achieving this peace with myself required me to first establish peace with food, very different from perfection with food, and this peace now overflows to the people in my life.

It was through eliminating trigger foods (which acted like drugs in my system) one day at a time and one meal at a time, developing a spiritual practice, and belonging to a supportive network that I was able to pick up the pieces of my childhood and use them to build a home for myself on the inside. I found food serenity, meaning I eat food to nourish and honor my body rather than "use" food to alter my mental state or achieve feelings of comfort, escape, or numbness. I grew to make peace with not only what I eat, even when I experience slips, but also with myself and those around me. It may sound impossible, but I know from experience that this food serenity is something you can achieve too.

Remember this, and say these words often and aloud:

The more peace I have with myself, the more peace I can have with everyone and everything around me.

Today, I lay my hand on my heart and turn inward to a place of unconditional love that lives contentedly inside me. It's a place of compassion, love, and kindness towards myself. It's a place that flourishes regardless of my weight or some unachievable, meaningless weight-loss goal.

I have heard from some that food addiction was the worst thing that could've happened to them. For those like my mother, it definitely was. For me, it has been a catalyst, a blessing if you will, to live a life with spiritual presence, movement, and enjoyment of whole foods.

Today, my mornings are very different. I awake in my beautiful, comfortable bed looking forward to my day, excited to start my day with my beautiful daughter. I begin each day with a spiritual practice: In the quiet of the morning, I take the time to be still, turn inward, and find my strength and magnificence. In my mind's eye, I envision the life I desire and sincerely give thanks for the tremendous blessings I have been given, which continue to flow into my life. *Then I start my day as though my prayers have already been answered.* I emerge from my bedroom a better person, a better mom. My cup is overflowing, and I have so much to give.

Though you may currently consider yourself a food addict, this label need not define you. By identifying your food triggers, establishing a wellness routine, and surrounding yourself with a supportive community, you can overcome your dependency on food. Diets may seem like the perfect solution to your food addiction, but I assure you their results are only temporary. Until you change your relationship with food, you cannot achieve lasting success.

The next chapter delves into the detrimental impact dieting can have on the mental, physical, and emotional wellbeing of recovering food addicts. Using scientific evidence, I unpack some of the manifold myths fed to us by the weight-loss industry and help you develop a healthier mindset about nutrition.

Chapter One Exercises

Exercise #1: Break Up with Your Scale

Examine your relationship with your scale. Is it neutral? Meaning, if you spent the last week eating on point and exercising, and your weight remains the same, or heaven forbid, you gain a pound—which, by the way, happens even when you do everything right—can you be neutral? Or does it make you want to throw in the towel?

It's always a red flag for me when a client adjusts her food intake to appease the scale. "How much can I eat without gaining weight? How much do I need to restrict to reach my goal-weight fast? I'm only going to eat this way so long as the scale keeps going down, but if it plateaus or dares go up a pound or two, I'm abandoning ship." These sentiments always make me sad. My client is completely missing the point. We eat whole, fresh foods because it feels amazing! Life feels different. We show up differently. We move our bodies every day because we are living organisms who need to exercise our flexibility, strength, and endurance to feel well. Stillness can potentially lead to illness.

You need and deserve a new measure of success. I always encourage my clients to measure non-scale victories to keep motivation high. Non-scale victories can include improved mood, energy, presence, and sleep; reduced need for medicines (with a doctor's approval); and regained ability to cross your legs or climb the stairs without experiencing pain or becoming winded. Become a detective for all the ways you're improving. When you can see you're winning, you'll want to keep going. Nothing slows you down more than discouragement.

I want you to consider whether your relationship with the scale is abusive:

1. Does the scale determine if it is going to be a good day or a bad day?
2. Does it dictate whether you are a good or bad person?
3. Does the number on the scale tell you what you should or shouldn't eat that day?
4. Is the scale your only measure of success?

If you answered yes to most of these questions, your relationship with the scale is toxic. It's time to cut ties and break up.

I get why your doctor, surgeon, and maybe even your pharmacist or dentist need to know what you weigh. But why do *you* need to know? If you're doing your best, eating whole foods, and moving your body, why does it matter what you weigh? Isn't your real job to love the body you have?

Take a few moments now to journal about the above questions:

Exercise #2: Identify Your Patterns

At what point did eating and your weight begin to feel like a problem in your life. This exercise will help you see patterns in your eating habits. Ask yourself:

1. What falsehoods did you believe about food or your body?
2. What messages did you hear, accept, and repeat about food or your body?
3. Which of these beliefs do you now need to let go of?

WHAT ARE YOUR BELIEFS ABOUT FOOD?

	BELIEFS ABOUT EATING FOOD	BELIEFS ABOUT YOUR WEIGHT	DO YOU STILL BELIEVE THIS? YES OR NO
0 - 5 YEARS OF AGE			
6 - 9 YEARS OF AGE			
10 - 12 YEARS OF AGE			
13 - 19 YEARS OF AGE			
20 - 29 YEARS OF AGE			
30 - 39 YEARS OF AGE			
40 + YEARS OF AGE			

Meet T.J.

Before taking Sandra's program, I was in a difficult and challenging marriage. After dating for ten years (yes, ten years!), my partner and I got married. The marriage highlighted my unhappiness with the person I married and the life I was living. I was actively binging as a coping mechanism, and before I knew it, I was binging pretty much every day of my marriage for six years. During this time, I was isolated from friends and family. Despite living with someone, I was lonely. Food became my ultimate solace—my lover, my best friend, my confidante. It was easy for me to turn to food for comfort, partly because this was a learned behavior for me, but especially because of my isolation.

My relationship with food was unstable from as far back as I can remember. My parents had very different ideologies on food. My mom was a part-time model and was very conscious of what she put in her body. She was continually on diets and constantly reading *Fit for Life*. She was strict with the foods I ate and categorized foods as "good" or "bad." My dad had a very laissez-faire relationship with food and ate whatever he wanted. My parents were separated, and from Monday to Friday, I stayed with my mom and ate in a very structured, intentional, and restrictive manner. After Halloween, my mother would lock my candy in a cabinet and give me two treats to add to my lunch from Monday to Friday. The candy lasted until summer.

From Friday evening until Sunday, I was with my dad, which felt like a celebratory holiday. I could eat whatever I wanted, and food was always on display. I continually ate to excess to counter my mom's restrictive ways of eating. All the foods my mom labeled as "bad" were readily available at my dad's house, and as soon as he parked in the driveway, I hopped out of the car and made a beeline for the kitchen to begin my weekend of non-stop eating. I didn't feel judged, I didn't feel scrutinized, and I could eat to my heart's content. I started binging in high school. After my mom passed away in 2003, I binged for a year and gained 100 pounds. During this time in my life, I felt I was merely surviving and not living.

The twenty-eight-day program helped me believe, for the first time, there was hope for recovery from food addiction. I finally felt seen and heard by Sandra and the community of participants in the program who will forever hold a very special place in my heart. Although I knew what self-compassion and self-love were in theory before joining the program, I couldn't authentically apply these skills until Sandra taught me how to incorporate them into my daily life.

The module on cravings in particular was a lightbulb moment for me. Previously, every single time I had a craving for a particular food, I ate it. The module on cravings shifted my mindset and showed me that just because I experience a craving doesn't mean I have to act on it. Furthermore, I learned my craving might not be an actual craving. It may be false hunger, or I may be thirsty. When I have a craving, I now reflect on it and, more often than not, realize I'm not hungry. I benefited from both the one-on-one and group coaching Sandra provided because each offered different perspectives on challenges I had faced, which ultimately helped me overcome them and thrive.

The module on neural pathways and behavior change exemplified the connection between my brain and why I engaged in overeating. I learned that behavior change is a process that takes time to develop, and this module highlighted the connection between my learned behavior and my brain. I still remember when Sandra said, "Wires that fire together, wire together!"

My life now has moved beyond feeling siloed, alone, and lonely with my thoughts to actively enjoying new experiences. Sandra's program was like seeing the sun burst from the clouds of my new lease on life.

Since taking the program, I have thrown out my scale (there was a time I thought I couldn't live without it), and I no longer diet. The freedom I feel is abundant, joyful, and refreshing. However, this would not have been possible without genuine self-love, which I learned in Sandra's program. My self-love journey was challenging, but Sandra's modules provided the foundation for me to rekindle the most important relationship I will ever have: the relationship with myself. I am no longer preoccupied with food, constantly thinking about what my next meal will be. I have found food neutrality and finally achieved peace with food. I am actively present in my life and create new opportunities for myself simply by expressing gratitude (which I also learned in the program), being open, and above all, being willing to try.

CHAPTER TWO

IF YOU WANT TO GAIN WEIGHT, GO ON A DIET

Tape Reel: My Sister's Wedding, SEPTEMBER 2001

"The diet will start tomorrow" is a lie that I've been living for fifteen years. Hundreds of tomorrows have gone by as my sister's wedding day draws nearer. My plan was to lose 100 pounds for her wedding. Now it's just two weeks away, and I am obviously not going to achieve this goal.

"Another failure," I thought. Yet again, I have set a goal to lose weight that I haven't accomplished. So, off I go to the dressmaker's to see if I can get a dress made in time for the big day. I despise walking into that store, but even more so, I loathe being measured.

With my head down, eyes focused on the heap of dark blue fabric in my hands, I ask her if she can get the job done. "Sure! No problem." But it will cost me $700. (And this was in 2001.) I am essentially asking her, "Just make me a tent so that my massive body has something to wear for my sist er's wedding, and then get me out of here." Instead, I say, "Yes, thank you. That will be fine." I quickly hurry out of my worst nightmare.

When I pick up the dress in time for my sister's wedding, it is a disheartening day. Sure, I am happy to have a dress that fits me, but to me, it is a truly horrific sight. I do give the dressmaker credit for a solid attempt to manufacture her best version of a Queen Anne jewel-cut dress, but the band had to be placed just below my chest, which was the smallest part of my body.

I, in my navy blue pavilion, under which sits all the weight of failure, stand beside my sister on her wedding day at the front of the church, in the greeting line at the banquet hall, and worst of all, on the dreaded dance floor.

I still have that dress. I keep it as a symbol of how far I have come. It represents a very sad part of my life: I don't just mean sad because of the unmanageability of my weight, but sad because of how much I truly despised myself at that time.

What I didn't know then is that diets don't work. My best intentions and my plans to diet were no match for the intensity of my cravings and urges to eat. It really never mattered which diet plan I tried—my only real struggle was cravings.

Cravings for me are intense, immediate, and overwhelming.

Giving into cravings affected my self-esteem and self-confidence. I would tell myself that I could start a new diet on Monday, that it would change my life.

But that Monday never came. There are more of those mythical Mondays than I can count. I was stuck in a loop of intensive urges to compulsively overeat and a mental tug of war to stop. One voice enticed me to give in, saying, "Just have one bite—you're in so much pain. You need this!" Then the voice of reason would say, "You can't keep doing this. You never stop at one. You'll feel awful when it's over!"

This back and forth was stressful and painful. Relief would wash over me when I'd tell myself that everything would be different tomorrow—which gave me permission to compulsively overeat today. I was perpetually waiting for the magical Monday morning—the morning I would wake up, eat clean, exercise, and set out on a path to lose a pound a day. Lose a pound a day—that's not even physiologically possible! Talk about setting myself up for failure!

Every compulsive overeating episode was followed by a personal attack on my psyche, and there was no way I could start a diet the next day. Instead, I would spend that next day trying to recuperate. That poor Monday morning never stood a chance.

If we set perfection as our standard for a weight-loss journey, then we're setting ourselves up to fail every time. I would start a new diet or program with a perfectionist attitude. I really believed that I would start at "Point A" and sail smoothly to my goal.

No mistakes and no detours.

However, the human experience looks nothing like that. Progress is really about taking three steps forward, one back, or four steps forward, two steps back, but ultimately moving forward.

The way I treated myself during a setback would determine whether I would achieve the life I wanted.

In the past, when I experienced a setback, I believed that if I took out the "shame stick" and beat myself up long and hard enough, I wouldn't make that mistake again. But nothing could be further from the truth. This harsh self-condemnation always led me to eat for comfort. I had to "flip the switch" each time I messed up with my eating. Those were the times I had to love myself most. Rather than condemning my slip, I needed to practice the utmost self-compassion because in that supportive environment, I could persevere and flourish.

Challenge yourself to look at a setback as a call for love.

❝ Every action a person performs is either an expression of love or a call for love. When people are kind, caring and compassionate, they are expressing love. When they are cruel, hurtful or mean (even to themselves), they are calling for love. Their mean actions are essentially saying, 'I need love.'"

– MARIANNE WILLIAMSON

Food Truths

My life, my experiences, my failures, and my triumphs have been my greatest teachers. They have taught me truths—truths about myself, truths about my eating habits, and truths about how the food industry markets ultra-processed foods despite how awful they make us feel. Many people believe we are living in an epidemic of addiction. Everyone seems to have a vice, whether it's food, shopping, drugs, alcohol, gaming, or even social media. The food addiction epidemic is likely due to processing. The more processed something is, the more addictive it is too, and we see this with various foods.

Let's look at the innocent coca leaf. There was a time in our history when perhaps someone chewed on a coca leaf and got a little spurt of energy to make it up the mountain or escape an attacking animal. Then we took that innocent coca leaf and processed it into cocaine, and then crack cocaine. The same could be said for the grape. The grape was your average innocent fruit, but what did humans do? Humans processed it and made it into wine. How many lives have been devastated by alcoholism?

I was at lunch with a colleague, and while he didn't have any food issues, he was very curious about food addiction because he'd gained about thirty pounds after becoming a dad and settling into domestic life. He asked, "Why do people give up bread? People have been eating bread for over ten thousand years. That's got to be fine," he said, and at that moment, our server set down a basket full of fluffy focaccia bread.

I never tell people what they should or shouldn't eat. It's not for me to say, but here's what I told him: "Bread is not the same as it was even a hundred years ago. My mother was born in the 1930's in Southern Italy, and one of her daily chores included baking bread for the family with real whole wheat, which was, in its entirety, unprocessed." My mother talked about having to eat that bread warm out of the oven because if we waited until the next day, it would be as hard as rock and difficult to eat. In fact, she soaked the bread in water the next day to make it edible. So I said to him, "If you could eat bread the way they did a hundred years ago, I'd say, 'Go ahead.' It would never be addictive. But that white fluffy focaccia bread? You know it's going to be addictive. It will hit the bliss point."

The "bliss point" is the term the food industry coined when they learned to combine the perfect quantities of sugar, salt, and fat. They know that with this perfect combination, they send your reward center over the moon. Any time your brain lights up in an unnatural way, addiction is possible.

High-fructose corn syrup was introduced to the market in the 1970's. With it, sugar became even more addictive and cost mere pennies to produce. High-fructose corn syrup is almost always a marker of poor quality, nutrient-free, disease-causing, industrial, food-like substances. With that said, I invite you to use this mantra whenever you're at a coffee shop or food court and trigger foods call your name:

My trigger foods are factory-made, poor quality, nutrient-free, disease-causing, industrial-made, food-like substances that have robbed me of joy and health.

Tape Reel: From Office to Home, JUNE 2000

I dread going home at night. I have a routine every night after leaving my office to try to cope with the discomfort I will find at home with my husband: I walk from my swanky downtown Toronto office to the nearest McDonald's and order a meal. But that's not enough, so I tell myself that I can have a kid's meal as well—that's not so bad. Afterwards, I walk to the subway. I am so saturated with salt and fat from the fast food that I have to switch to something sweet, and so I grab a chocolate bar. I eat the chocolate bar, and maybe another, until it is all too sweet, even for me. I change trains at Bloor-Yonge Station, and I need a bag of chips—I need the crunch and saltiness. So I grab one at the convenience stand next to the tracks.

I now understand that this type of eating is called "food cycling." Food cycling allowed me to "use" food in greater amounts. I would cycle between sugar to the point where I couldn't stand it and then crave salt and fat to take the edge off. Once I overdid it on the salt, I would switch back to the sugar. It was my cycle of hell.

The first thing I always do after walking into my house is reach under my shirt and rip off my bra. Somehow it had become so much tighter and was now digging into my bloated chest to the point where it was tormenting my skin. My waistline is often just as bad, indented and red around my belly button from my clothing. Finally, I dissolve into the couch and pacify myself with whatever is on television, completely numb from the pain of my life and bloated with self-hatred—until my husband asks, "Do you want dinner?" to which I answer, "Of course."

This lifestyle wholly affected my life, and not for the better. It led me to require a daily cocktail of mood stabilizers and antidepressants by age twenty-nine. And no matter which pharmaceuticals I ingested, I still depended on the drug of ultra-processed foods, which inevitably caused my mood to plummet regardless.

If even one area of my life was highly dysfunctional, toxic, or painful, I wanted to use food for comfort. It was almost ridiculous for me to believe that I could stay in a horrible marriage, continue my severely codependent relationship with my mom, and somehow also stop eating for comfort.

It was only a matter of time before I came to a crossroads and was forced to choose one of two options: Do the internal work to change my outer world OR continue living an unhealthy and unhappy life. Using food was how I stayed stuck. I never stood a chance so long as I was in it.

The Drivers of Eating

When it comes to eating, there are two parts of your brain that drive you. One part, the biological drive, tells you that you need to eat to stay alive. The other part is the desire drive, or the hedonic drive, and it has nothing to do with our biological need for food.

When we talk about hunger and feeling satiated, we need to talk about **ghrelin, leptin,** and **insulin. Ghrelin** is a hormone that is released when your stomach starts to empty. It sends a message to your brain saying, "Listen up! Pay attention! It's time to eat." When you ignore it—which we've all done—more ghrelin is released. This is why when you experience the feeling of being "hangry," you lose focus. Suddenly, the reason you were ignoring these signals—the project, the email, whatever else you may have been working on—is forgotten. There's no focus left for that project or email, and your body is telling you, "Hey! It's time to eat!" This is normal, but it's important to listen to this hormone before it ends up attacking you.

Leptin is a hormone released from fat cells. It signals to the brain, "We've had enough. We're full. We can push away the plate. We're satisfied and satiated." Leptin does not affect food intake from meal to meal. Instead, it acts to alter food intake and control energy expenditure over the long term.

Finally, **insulin** is probably something you're more familiar with than the previous two hormones. Insulin is the hormone that controls the glucose levels in your body, and it is essential that this hormone be regulated. Having elevated insulin levels is unhealthy for a lot of reasons, and we know that refined sugar and flour—which are found in countless products on grocery store shelves—are products that raise insulin.

I'm a fan of Dr. Robert Lustig. He's an American pediatric endocrinologist and the author of *Fat Chance: Beating the Odds Against Sugar, Processed Food, Obesity, and Disease.*[2] He theorizes that when elevated insulin runs through our bloodstreams, it may prevent leptin from reaching our brains, blocking the message to stop eating.

Tape Reel: My Childhood Corner Store, OCTOBER 1982

My mom walks me home from school each day. I leave the only place I feel safe—a place where, if I work hard, someone will see and praise me—only to return to a house filled with chaos. Evenings are scary in my home, but food helps me through it. On the

---

[2]   Robert H. Lustig, *Fat Chance: Beating the Odds Against Sugar, Processed Food, Obesity, and Disease.* New York: Penguin, 2013.

way home, my mom and I stop at the corner store, which acts as the retail version of my childhood "drug dealer." I can get anything I need to make it through the night. I can smooth the loneliness, and I can numb the pain. My holy trinity consists of chips, Tab soda, and chocolate Cherry Blossoms. I have learned that food is my consolation prize for the childhood that never was, the life unlived, and all the missed opportunities.

For many, many years, I feel as if my "I'm full" switch has been forever broken. In fact, in my twenties, I couldn't stop eating until I felt physically ill. What I don't yet understand is that my body and my brain will never be satisfied with ultra-processed foods. I have an abnormal response to refined sugar and refined flour; ingesting these foods causes me to want more. Natural whole foods, however, react in my body in natural ways. The chewing, the fiber, and the nutrients allow me to feel satisfied.

Over time, as you abstain from your trigger foods, you'll gradually achieve appetite correction and a peaceful relationship with food where you consume it for nourishment. You'll honor your body. No longer will you "use" food like a drug to alter your mental state or achieve a feeling.

The Desire to Eat

The desire to eat has nothing to do with hunger. Think back to your last Thanksgiving gathering. If your family is anything like mine, you had way too much food. Afterwards, people were lying on the couch and floor with belt buckles undone, taking short, shallow breaths. Then someone says, "The warm pumpkin pie is served!" and everyone gets up, suddenly finding room for dessert. Where does this room come from? Their bodies are literally screaming at them to stop. We can't eat any more, but somehow we manage to fit in dessert. *This* is the desire to eat, and it arises primarily from the feel-good neurochemical called dopamine.

Dopamine is the neurochemical of desire and wanting. This desire produces action (e.g., getting off the couch and moving towards the dessert even though you're beyond full). Dopamine is also the neurochemical of anticipation. Food addicts often say that ordering a pizza and waiting for its arrival bring about greater anticipation and excitement than actually eating the pizza. Lastly, dopamine is the neurochemical of learning. When you're experiencing intense pleasure from chemically-engineered foods that have been manufactured to overwhelm your reward center, your brain takes a "snapshot" of exactly what's happening. It notes the location, colors, smells, tastes, sounds, and company surrounding you in that blissful moment. When the scenario is repeated, your brain will want those foods again. So in early recovery, when you're in a familiar situation where compulsive overeating has occurred hundreds of times (e.g., sitting on the sofa late at night, all alone), this scene can trigger you to want to eat, even if you're not hungry and have chosen food sobriety. Plan for these high-risk times, change up your routines, switch rooms, and find high-value activities to replace the feelings that comfort food used to provide.

When we talk about food addiction, dopamine is such an important neurochemical, so I want to spend an extra moment on it with you. The following quote from the NAADAC will help you understand how your food addiction may have progressed from early stage to middle stage, and even late stage:

> Highly palatable foods saturate the brain with so much dopamine that it eventually adapts by desensitizing itself, reducing the number of cellular receptors that recognize and respond to the neurochemical. Consequently, the brains of overeaters demand a lot more sugar and fat to reach the same threshold of pleasure once experienced with smaller amounts of food. These people may, in fact, continue to overeat as a way of recapturing, or even maintaining, a sense of wellbeing.[3]

For me, near the end of my overeating career, I would dig into a pizza and the first bite would be euphoric. Then the next few bites were…good. And then after the first slice, the pizza was just okay. I wasn't enjoying it anymore, but I just kept eating. I would eat the whole thing. I could not stop. My brain was desensitized to dopamine.

I often hear from my clients in early recovery that their meal plan doesn't give them a buzz. They weren't hungry, and they didn't want more real food; they wanted their reward center to be tantalized.

Eliminating your trigger foods might leave what feels like a void in your life, but it's important to fill this void with a life of meaning, anticipation, and appreciation. This will supply the missing dopamine your brain is seeking, the dopamine that your trigger foods once supplied.

It has been said that the opposite of addiction is connection. Actively seeking a support network, such as fellowship opportunities or service work, is a good

---

[3]   National Association for Alcoholism and Drug Abuse Counselors, 2016 Annual Conference, Milestones Eating Disorders Program.

way to replace addiction with connection. You can also assemble a toolkit of alternative sources for releasing those feel-good neurochemicals without food, such as exercising, singing, laughing, meditating, spending time in nature, and building a community of people you can count on. As adults who no longer use food for comfort, we must develop other self-soothing routines.

The Dangers of Restrictive Dieting

Getting to a healthy body size isn't *just* about the food. I'm suggesting that making better food choices may have very little to do with the food itself, but rather a daily diet of nurturing and caring for your body, mind, and spirit.

I want you to answer the three following questions:

- Do you have a history of chronic dieting and restricting? (e.g., Do you have a past filled with crazy diets and attempts to lose weight quickly?)
- What percentage of your diet is ultra-processed foods or fast and convenient foods?
- Do you have some faulty thinking patterns when it comes to eating? (e.g., Do you binge and then restrict?)

Restrictive Diets and Metabolic Damage

If you want to gain weight, you should go on a diet.

There's research that proves over ninety percent of people who go on diets, especially restrictive ones, gain the weight back—and sometimes more.

In my mid-twenties, I landed a job at an international consulting firm, my chance to work on Bay Street in Toronto. So I hired a Bay Street weight-loss expert. It was June when I started her program. I remember the feeling I got when she promised I would be fifty pounds lighter by Christmas. I was sold! Whatever money they wanted, I was handing it over—I desperately wanted to be thin. At the time, I didn't know it would be the last diet I ever went on.

I was put on a restrictive diet and managed to stick to it for six months, and I lost fifty pounds. I also managed to kick-start the starvation mode in my brain. This is a real thing, often referred to as "metabolic damage." It is your body's natural response to long-term calorie restriction. Unbeknownst to me, a cascade of events was happening in my brain that would drive me to seek food and eat food—and not just any food.

Our brains are efficient, and my brain drove me to consume calorie-dense, sugary foods. This drive is what kept our ancestors alive during famines. My brain had no idea I was in a self-imposed famine (my restrictive diet). My brain believed it was a life-or-death event, and it sent messages to me to eat. *Every famine is followed by a feast.*

My rebound not only included gaining back the fifty pounds I lost, but adding another fifty pounds in a little over a year. It was one of the most humiliating experiences of my life—to show up at work heavier and heavier, month after month. I believed it was my fault, and I hated myself for it.

Make a promise to yourself that you'll never again go on a restrictive diet. End the famine/feast cycle. We know that over ninety percent of diets fail. Would you ever get on a plane with a ninety percent chance of crashing?

The Dangers of Eating Processed Foods

For tens of thousands of years, humans have been able to regulate our eating and our weight, but in the last seventy years or so, something has gone wrong. It was likely the introduction of ultra-processed foods.

Ultra-processed foods are chemically engineered food-like substances made in factories. They are nutrient-poor and cause disease. My sincere hope is that you shift your perspective, that you no longer romanticize your trigger foods or yearn for them. I hope that you see real food, food that comes from the earth, as the only food you want to eat, and that you see your trigger foods as chemically-engineered foods that have robbed you of health, emotional stability, and opportunities. I want you to attach a huge price tag to your trigger foods so you never feel that you're missing out.

From today forward, I invite you to select foods that give you energy, vitality, and clarity of mind so that you can live your best life. I'm not here to villainize any particular food. In fact, I want you to have a peaceful relationship with food. Ultra-processed foods and sugary foods often ignite the hunt for more and more ultra-processed and sugary foods. They drive up hunger and cravings. Many people today have chosen a sugar-free life, not because they identify as food addicts or because they struggle with eating or their weight, but because they understand the damaging effects of sugar.

The Dangers of Faulty Thinking Patterns

One of the greatest obstacles in my weight-loss journey was faulty thinking—the mental obsession with food and the addiction loop it creates. I was stuck in an addiction loop for over ten years.

The loop would begin with the thought, "I'm just going to have one bite." I would tell myself, "I'm just going to have a paper-thin sliver of cake," and then I would eat a large slice. I would think, "Oh, I've totally blown it. I might as well go back and get seconds, thirds, and everything else." I would then tell myself, "The diet starts tomorrow." This is the single greatest lie I've ever told myself, a lie that played on repeat for much of my life.

I would feel the overwhelming cravings, the urges to overeat. I didn't know how to manage the panic of wanting to eat compulsively. Then relief would wash over me; I would start the diet tomorrow. I told myself tomorrow would be different, but today I needed to *use* food. Starting tomorrow, I would eat salad every day, I would lose a pound a day, I would even chart my weight-loss, a formula doomed to fail every time. That tomorrow never came—today is tomorrow. It's always today—you'll always have this moment to choose differently.

Escape the Addiction Loop

Now, the best way to escape the addiction loop and build new neural pathways is to let go of perfectionism. Letting go of the idea of "I need to eat perfectly" allows you to never have to start over. Instead, you see your moments of compulsive overeating as little bleeps or mistakes. In fact, I've started calling these mistakes *calls for love*. So when I eat in ways that I didn't want to or I'm not proud of, I reframe it as my *call for love* because, in this moment, I know I need self-love, compassion, understanding, and nurturing. And interestingly enough, when I began to understand this addiction loop behavior and that I needed to be ultra kind to myself, I actually began to make better decisions about my eating habits. Be kind, gentle, and nurturing to yourself. Why? Because we all succeed in this kind of environment.

When you're gentle with yourself, you give yourself the opportunity to do better, to be better. And it's one of the quickest routes to healing and improving your self-esteem and growing your self-love. It's important to understand that you are a physical being, a mental being, and a spiritual being who needs a plan of care for each part of you.

Now that I've likely shattered your understanding of diets and the role they play in your weight-loss journey, I will equip you with alternative, healthier strategies for losing weight and gaining food serenity. In the next chapter, we'll dive deeper into the first of the Three Pillars of Food Addiction Recovery to help transform your tumultuous relationship with food to one of gratitude, nourishment, and ultimately peace.

Chapter Two Exercises

Exercise #1: In What State Are You Eating?

I've never been a fan of food journaling; the act is always so triggering for me. I was happy to record everything I ate when I was "perfect." However, when I compulsively overate, it felt too humiliating to record what I was eating, much less share it with another person.

In this journal, don't be too concerned about the food, though it will offer clues to your eating triggers. This exercise is more about discovering your personal patterns of eating that are both helpful and unhelpful.

As you consistently collect data on when you eat, why you eat, and what you eat, you will begin to understand what drives you to eat. You will gain the most valuable information when you record meals that have not gone according to plan. Drop the judgment if you want to find true answers and solutions.

When recording the times at which you eat, pay attention to the number of hours between meals and how that affects your hunger level at each meal and the food choices you make. When recording your Emotional State prior to a meal, begin noticing themes among circumstances that lead you to consume food for comfort or escape. When recording your Emotional State after a meal, try to recognize trends that may help you better understand your relationship with food.

Here is an example of how to record:

TIME	8AM	1PM	6PM	8PM
MEAL	BREAKFAST	LUNCH	DINNER	SNACK
EMOTIONAL STATE BEFORE MEAL NEUTRAL, CONTENT, BORED, LONELY, SAD, GUILTY, STRESSED, ANGRY...				
HUNGER LEVEL (1-5) BEFORE MEAL 1- RAVENOUS 2- REASONABLE 3-NEUTRAL 4- COMFORTABLE 5- FULL TO THE POINT OF FEELING ILL				
FOOD(S) EATEN				
HUNGER LEVEL (1-5) AFTER MEAL				
EMOTIONAL STATE AFTER MEAL NEUTRAL, CONTENT, BORED, LONELY, SAD, GUILTY, STRESSED, ANGRY...				

Meet Kathleen

My life before Sandra's twenty-eight-day program was frustrating. I had dieted on and off from ages seventeen to sixty-eight. I had tried almost every diet created, each with their own promise of weight-loss and "maintenance" where the weight magically stays off. These diets always worked initially but ended badly.

The diet roller coaster I was on kept speeding along. The tracks it followed always took the same twisting turns. It began with me rigidly sticking to the diet: "This time it would be different," I swore. The journey would start with strict adherence to the menu. It was one of deprivation, hunger, obsession, cravings, binging, and starving to make up for it.

My progress was always measured by the number on the scale. If the needle went down, I was rewarded, if it went up, I was reprimanded. The struggle continued, and then, finally, I would achieve my goal weight. I had succeeded because the scale said so. There was no elation on my part.

The diet came to an end and maintenance began. This was the beginning of a frantic attempt to keep that number on the scale exactly the same. Maintaining my new weight was total hell. Feelings of desperation, panic, rage, and helplessness crept in. The strain was too much. I lost total control and gorged on anything and everything. I could not stop eating. I would then quit my diet and proceed to eat uncontrollably until I surpassed my starting weight.

I felt like a total failure and would hide in shame; I did not understand why I wasn't successful when others were. Finally, I could not stand myself any longer. The scale was always screaming at me. My brain was foggy and confused. I was eating to numb the pain of being overweight, which only added to my existing weight. I realized what I was doing and how ridiculous it was, but I could not stop and did not know why.

My internal environment was negative and angry. The nagging voice in my head kept saying the weight had to come off, my cardiologist begged me to get the weight off, my A1C was climbing. There wasn't a shred of gentle, positive feeling or love for myself to be found.

Fast forward to Sandra's twenty-eight-day program. I wanted off the diet roller coaster so I could finally achieve peace with food. At this point, I did not care if I ever lost another pound. I just wanted it to stop. I didn't understand that I was a food addict or even know what food addiction was. I did not understand how the brain reacted to my trigger foods or why.

When I started detoxing from my trigger foods, I realized that food addiction was real. I could not ingest my trigger foods without causing chemical changes, which resulted in a total loss of control—a tail spin into the depths of binge eating. As odd as it may sound, this realization was a huge relief for me. No other diet I tried even mentioned food addiction, much less explained the physiology and chemistry of addiction. I knew that if they did, they would not have thousands of repeat dieters who fail their programs and then pointlessly try again. Imagine the financial loss they'd suffer if their plans actually worked.

Once I completed the detox from my trigger foods, I felt calmer and clearer. The fuzzy brain was gone. My frustration eased, and I could finally internalize what I was learning. I now live peacefully with food and have even gone down a few sizes in clothing, though I have no idea what I weigh.

Today, I have and continue to build a great "tool box." I have embraced the checklist and my daily routine. I often return to my notes, my list of daily successes, and my journals. Though I struggled most with mirror work, I know I would have never learned to respect myself without it. I also use the list of non-negotiables frequently. No matter what happens, even if I binge, I understand that I still deserve self-love and compassion. And last but not least, I rely on my recovery community because I know they understand me in ways no one else can.

Sandra is an inspiration who has walked in her clients' shoes. My advice to anyone interested in embarking on their own twenty-eight-day journey is this: This course will change you. If you decide to take it, know that you will not be judged. Ask yourself if you are willing to make a firm twenty-eight-day commitment. Keep an open mind, honestly do the exercises, contact your accountability buddy every day, and try not to miss a session. This course and the community surrounding it may be the only true solution to rampant obesity because they enable you to gain peace within yourself. But you have to do it for you.

CHAPTER THREE

MAKING PEACE WITH FOOD

Three Pillars of Food Addiction Recovery

The day you start using food to cope with life is the day you begin to stunt your emotional maturity, and this is exactly what I did until the age of thirty. My only mechanism for coping with and managing the things life threw my way—bad grades, breakups, mistakes at work, memories of past trauma—was eating until the pain was entirely numbed. When I finally decided to end my destructive relationship with food, I felt stripped of my comfort but also completely maladjusted to life. I didn't understand how to navigate situations that seemed so easy for my peers. With tremendous support and by becoming a spiritual seeker, I learned about the importance of being at peace with myself, at peace with food, and ultimately at peace with the people in my life. Achieving food serenity is about returning food to its rightful purpose. Food is meant to nourish and honor our bodies. We begin the journey and stop using it as a drug to numb our pain.

There are many roads to recovery. However, through my many years of experience working with thousands of people who identify as food addicts, I have found that a few strategies in particular work for most every client.

The Three Pillars of Food Addiction Recovery make up an action plan to eliminate trigger foods, develop mindfulness and spirituality, and find a support network. I want you to think of the pillars as a three-legged stool. If you neglect one of the legs, the stool will collapse.

Creating a foundation for the pillars is an important first step: Create an internal environment that is kind, gentle, and nurturing. It is hard to change positively when motivated by shame, guilt, or hate. The first brave step in your recovery journey is learning to unconditionally accept yourself as you are today. Acceptance and self-love should be unwavering, meaning the love doesn't change when you lose weight. That is true, unconditional, energizing love, love that will sustain you along the road to food serenity.

> **"**I have never seen a person grow or change in a self-constructive meaningful way when motivated by guilt, shame, or self-hate."
>
> – HERB GOLDBERG

To help you recover from addictive eating and ultimately achieve food serenity— and peace with yourself—I will repeat these three pillars throughout this book because repetition is the only form of permanence. Even when things are going well—and especially if they are not—I encourage you to continue to return to the three pillars.

You hold in your hands the guideposts needed to take this journey for yourself. Even if you fall off the wagon, so long as you keep coming back to these pillars, you will feel my love and support for you emanate off the pages.

Remember, becoming your best self is not a race against others but a spiritual and enlightening journey you take to achieve peace with yourself, with your body, and with the people in your life.

Three Pillars Of Food Addiction Recovery

Pillar One: Eliminate Trigger Foods

What Classifies a Food as a Trigger Food?

Trigger foods are often factory-made, nutrient-poor, disease-causing foods chemically engineered to overwhelm the pleasure center of our brains. For those of us who identify as food addicts, we crave these foods and cannot stop eating them, even if we suffer consequences from our eating or our weight that we desperately do not want. These industrial foods, or "food-like substances," are foods that we obsess about. Once we start eating a trigger food, it is difficult to stop or have a reasonable portion. Consuming your trigger foods often leads to an overeating episode that involves more ultra-processed foods. These foods almost always contain refined sugar, refined flour, and have been heavily processed.

It has been said a miracle is a "shift in perception." My sincere desire for you is that you have a shift in perception around your trigger foods. I hope that you see whole foods as real food, and you see your trigger foods, not as treats or comfort, but as chemically engineered, "food-like substances" that have robbed you of the life you've always wanted. These "food-like substances" come with an enormous price tag. You've paid an emotional, physical, and spiritual price for eating trigger foods, but you're done with that.

In his book *The End of Overeating*, which I highly recommend, David Kessler explains what is happening within the food industry. He writes, "Right now, the food industry is not only generating billions of dollars by designing hyper-palatable combinations of sugar, fat, and salt, but also creating products that can rewire our brains, driving us to eat more and more of those products."[4]

Now, you may ask yourself, "Why would the food industry want to do that? Why would they want to make food addictive?" Well, it's quite simple. They want the greatest share of your wallet. Unfortunately, we live in a world where most people live under the veil of delusion. The veil normalizes our consumption of addictive foods. It convinces us that these foods are "treats" that can actually be good for us in moderation, but this couldn't be further from the truth for food addicts. In the end, a trigger food is a drug that hits your bliss point and overwhelms the reward center of your brain, making you want even more. Many people who don't identify as food addicts and don't struggle with their weight have still chosen a sugar-free lifestyle. Why? Because eating whole, natural foods brings health, vitality, clear-mindedness, presence, and the list goes on and on.

Again, trigger foods can be defined as foods that are usually refined, processed, and man-made. These are the foods that you obsess about, eat to excess, and often, once you start eating them, cannot stop consuming. Sometimes, eating these foods may lead to a binge, and it may become difficult for you to connect the dots about why you can't stop craving these foods.

---

4   David A. Kessler, *The End of Overeating: Taking Control of the Insatiable North American Appetite.* Toronto: McClelland & Stewart, 2010.

Now, it's important to address some mental blocks you may experience as you decide to heal your addictive eating. It's important to eliminate your personal trigger foods—but I know what you're thinking: "I can't do this for the rest of my life. I can't not eat birthday cake ever again. I can't commit to that." Well, here's the thing: I can't commit to anything for the rest of my life either. So here's what I want you to understand. When that voice in your head says, "I can't do this forever," say, "You're right."

No one can commit to the rest of their life. I don't even know what's going to happen in five years. I don't even know what will happen in five days, but change begins with self-efficacy. Self-efficacy is the belief that you can do this, and this belief is important for sustaining long-term behavioral change. Often, when we think of a lifelong commitment, our self-efficacy will be very low. When you ask yourself if one meal is possible, your self-efficacy will likely be high. I need—and you need—your self-efficacy to remain high. Please don't entertain thoughts of what the rest of your life will look like.

Here's a game I would play to keep my self-efficacy high. It's called *I Won't Today, But I Might Tomorrow*. I would tell myself, "I'm not going to compulsively overeat today, but if I wake up tomorrow morning and want to, I'm going to." This thinking process would help me get through an overwhelming urge to overeat. It's a powerful strategy that I invite you to try. Every day I delayed compulsive overeating, I got stronger and rewired my brain, lifting the craving fog in which ultra-processed foods had me trapped. Every day I delayed my drive to compulsively overeat, I strengthened my self-efficacy, and every day, things got a little easier.

If you're anything like me, I tried for years to lose weight. I would try and fail and try again and fail again. Wanting something so badly and experiencing continuous failure, I began to believe I was the failure. You may be thinking to yourself, "Okay, I'm a few chapters into this book, but I've tried so many things and have always failed, and this is probably something else I will fail at." I'm here to tell you the truth. You are not a failure. You haven't failed. Instead, the diets have failed you. Diets were never going to work. You have been on the wrong treatment plan. That's no different than if you went to a doctor and were diagnosed with diabetes but were then sent for chemotherapy.

This is what happens to food addicts. We are given diets, restrictions, and moderations, but all they do is keep us stuck in the addiction loop. Instead, surround yourself with people who, like you, get up each morning and try to hit the bull's-eye with their recovery. Some days you'll hit the mark, and it will feel wonderful. When you miss, you can lean into your community for unconditional love and support. Sometimes, you will fall down, but eventually, you will reach a place where the pillars of recovery are built into your daily life. Having eliminated trigger foods and connected to a supportive community, you're ready to dive into the beautiful world of developing your spirituality and mindfulness towards not only your relationship with food but your whole life.

Let's say you're out to dinner with a loved one. The server places a breadbasket at the center of the table. Now, if you say yes to the breadbasket and tell yourself that it's okay because bread isn't a trigger food, what you're not realizing is the effect that those slices of bread will have on your body. What you're not realizing is that those slices will actually spike your hunger and cravings, causing you to order a pasta dish, and then dessert, and ultimately end up at home, rummaging through the cupboards wanting more. Afterwards, you may think, "Wait. How did I get here?" And the bread likely won't come to mind. But there is actually a link between bread and craving more starchy/sugary foods.

Together, one day at a time, one meal at a time, we can eliminate our trigger foods. We step onto this path paved with self-love and are guided by our inner wisdom. Our understanding of the steps will develop moment by moment, and we will stop fighting and fearing food. We will move away from the "must-do's" and "can't haves" of eating and learn to select food using our inner knowledge, a place of perfect peace.

Get to Know Your Addict Voice

I've been working with food addicts for over twenty years, and what I know for sure is that a craving is *always a lie*. There is never a good reason to consume trigger foods. I had to learn to recognize my addict voice and become familiar with the lies it told me so I would stop falling for them.

In Canada, there's a scam where fraudulent callers claim they are from the CRA (Canada Revenue Agency). People get scared and give the fraudulent callers their personal financial information, and you can guess what happens next. The Canadian media has done a great job educating everyone about this fraud so no one else falls victim to it.

I often get these calls, and the moment I hear the "lie," I hang up.

I want you to get there with your addict voice. The moment you begin to hear the lie, hang up!

So let's get clear on what the lies are. Most people have about three to five top lies when it comes to cravings. They generally sound like the ones listed below:

- "Have one bite; you can handle it."
- "Don't worry, you will start the diet tomorrow."
- "You deserve a treat."
- "It's too hard to eat right today. I'm too stressed, too sad, nothing is going my way."
- "You have to have it! When will you get to eat this kind of food again?"

Sometimes the voice is demanding, urgent. Sometimes it's harsh and critical. For some, the voice is very seductive.

Understand—Separate—Breathe

Let me show you how to stay calm and confident when faced with an overwhelming craving or urge to compulsively overeat. I've created a Three-Step Cognitive Behavioral Therapy (a CBT hack if you will) to help you manage cravings.

1. Understand: Cravings Are Lies

The first thing you should do when experiencing a craving is acknowledge that it is a lie—and it's always a lie. There is no good reason to have trigger foods that have robbed you of health, joy, and opportunities.

2. Separate Yourself From the Voice

The next step is to separate yourself from the addict voice inside your head. Instead of listening to this voice and thinking it is *you*, recognize the craving as a glitch in your brain. It's important to know that addiction touches four parts of the brain: the reward center, the habit center, the stress center, and the euphoric recall center. Start to separate yourself from the craving and understand where it comes from.

For example, let's say you've watched a fast-food commercial that has set your dopamine soaring. You might tell yourself, "I've got to have it! It's been such a stressful day!" You have enough evidence to prove that a fast-food meal is only pleasurable while you are eating it. The moment the last bite is swallowed, everything changes in an instant. The remorse, bitterness, and feelings of hopelessness quickly replace the euphoria of the meal. Once you spot this lie, you can ask yourself, "What just happened?" and get to the bottom of what part of your brain this craving ignited.

In that moment, ask yourself this:

- *Is it the reward center?* Do I want to experience the momentary pleasure of the trigger food?
- *Is it the habit center?* Am I used to eating something sweet at three o'clock every day?
- *Is it the stress center?* Do I feel overwhelmed and believe eating will soothe me?
- *Is it the euphoric recall center?* Am I tempted to eat something I already know tastes amazing?

For food addicts, oftentimes, a craving feels like a demand but it's important to learn to separate yourself from the craving. Remember, you are not the addict voice in your head telling you that you *need* to eat this.

3. Breathe

The final step in the CBT technique is breath work. Because cravings can cause anxiety, taking ten deep, grounding breaths will oxygenate your frontal lobe and help you make better decisions. These breaths will slowly drown out the addict voice and allow you to reject the lies your brain is telling you about what you should eat.

When committing to this CBT technique, it's important to start out with low-risk situations and then slowly work your way up to high-risk situations. So I want to ask you to do a little homework—not for me, but for yourself—and it's important. I want you to sit down and write out the top lies your addict voice uses to get you to eat in a way that you really don't want to. Then I want you to memorize them so you can identify and dismiss them as they come into your head. Finally, I want you to carry this three-step technique with you. Put it on your fridge, take a picture on your smartphone, and carry it around with you. The point of this homework is to help you practice identifying the lies, separating yourself from them, and breathing to let go of them.

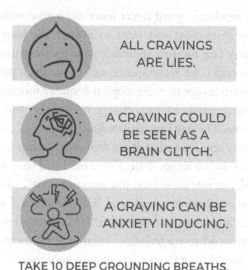

ALL CRAVINGS ARE LIES.

A CRAVING COULD BE SEEN AS A BRAIN GLITCH.

A CRAVING CAN BE ANXIETY INDUCING.

TAKE 10 DEEP GROUNDING BREATHS.

Plan—Prepare—Protect

Now, you probably recognize plan, prepare, and protect as part of emergency and disaster preparedness, but it easily translates to your relationship with food, cravings, and yourself. The best way I can put it is as follows: "How will you Plan—Prepare—Protect your recovery at this moment?"

When it comes to your Food Addiction Recovery, it's important to not only ignore the craving lies your brain tells you but also to plan, prepare, and protect yourself from the cravings you'll have. Planning, preparing, and protecting, combined with the three-step CBT technique, will help you stay calm and confident in the face of a craving—and it's all about practice. Like a firefighter practices saving lives in simulated emergencies so they know exactly what to do when faced with an actual burning building, you too must practice fighting off cravings before they hit.

Regardless of what stage of your recovery you are in, loving yourself as you are and having daily routines and rituals will sustain you.

When you have a newborn, you'd never leave the house without diapers, extra clothing, and formula because you want to protect the baby's wellbeing at all costs. This is the way you need to approach your recovery too. And you can do this using the three-step CBT technique as well as the three pillars.

It took me time to accept that the magical Monday morning with the perfect diet that would change my behaviors, change my weight, and ultimately change me would never come. The day I surrendered my weight to God was the day I was finally able to end my abusive and codependent relationship with the scale. It was mostly lies anyway. I had to let go. With all the lies I had been telling myself—the "I'll start tomorrow, just one more bite, just one more slice"—how was I supposed to know the difference between truth and lies? How was I supposed to know when I *needed* to eat and when I *desired* to eat? If I continued down the path I was on, looking to food to achieve a feeling—whether numbing out, relieving stress, or feeling love—I would have faced a fate like my mother's.

These are all things I know you can achieve too. I know you can stay calm and confident in the face of cravings and put an end to your destructive eating habits. It all requires self-love, self-compassion and practice in these key points:

- Cravings are always lies.

- There is never a good reason to "use" food.

- If you can get familiar with your addict voice and recognize its lies, you never have to fall for them again.

- Most importantly, you are enough to overcome the wave of cravings.

Starting today, any time you experience a setback with food, don't see it as a mistake. Instead, see it as a call for love because that's what it is. You're calling for love in those moments you seek solace in food. This love you seek is available to you, and you can give it to yourself. In fact, we come from love and we *are* love. Only you can withhold it from yourself and put conditions on it. Consider this: *What if the missing piece has always been unconditional love for yourself?*

Now that you are learning to identify and conquer your cravings, we will cultivate a spirituality and mindfulness practice that enables you to achieve peace with food and yourself. The next chapter focuses on the second of the Three Pillars of Food Addiction Recovery and unpacks the manifold benefits of developing a daily spirituality practice that will enable you to connect with yourself as a means for overcoming your dependency on food.

Chapter Three Exercises

Exercise #1: Identify Your Trigger Foods

Write down your addictive foods or trigger foods. These are foods that you obsess about. Once you start eating a trigger food, it is very difficult to stop or have a reasonable portion. Eating your trigger foods often leads to an overeating episode containing other foods. These foods almost always contain refined sugar and refined flour.

Ask yourself:

- What do I eat when I experience strong emotions? (i.e., anger, sadness, stress, excitement, happiness.)
- What is the personal price I've paid for continuing to eat addictive foods?
- What price have I paid physically, emotionally, and spiritually?
- What have trigger foods robbed me of?
- What opportunities have I lost?
- What are my behaviors that lead to overeating? (i.e., eating in front of a screen, eating in the car, eating standing up at the kitchen counter.)

Hint: You can keep it simple. You may notice that all your trigger foods contain refined sugar and refined flour, or have been deep fried. Please keep in mind, some trigger foods don't have sugar or flour (i.e., chips, which is one of the most addictive foods on the planet). Make sure to list those foods as well.

_____

_____

_____

_____

_____

Exercise #2: Identify Your Lies

What are the top five lies your addict voice uses when you have a craving? Examples below:

- Have one bite—you can handle it.
- Don't worry, you will start the diet tomorrow.
- It's too hard to eat right today. You are too stressed, too sad, and nothing is going your way.
- You deserve a treat.

_____

_____

_____

_____

_____

Exercise #3: Manage Your Cravings

Refer to the three-step CBT (Cognitive Behavior Therapy) technique when you need it. I suggest taking a picture of the technique or printing it so you can easily focus on the steps in a high-risk situation and effectively manage your cravings.

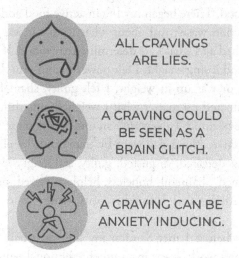

ALL CRAVINGS ARE LIES.

A CRAVING COULD BE SEEN AS A BRAIN GLITCH.

A CRAVING CAN BE ANXIETY INDUCING.

TAKE 10 DEEP GROUNDING BREATHS.

Meet Andrea

In a few weeks, I will turn fifty-one. When I look back over my life, food and what it has represented to me, quickly comes to mind. Food—and my relationship with it—has been an incredibly significant part of my life. It has quite literally been my greatest source of pleasure, purpose, and pain. It has given me my highest highs and taken me to my lowest lows. It has sometimes served as my only source of connection to others and yet has also forced me into utter isolation. It's been complicated to say the least.

I first remember food becoming the main focus of my life at age six when, rather suddenly that summer, I went from being a thin child to a chubby child. I recall the doctor sending me to see a nutritionist and as a result, having to abide by *Canada's Food Guide*. This was essentially a diet that included measuring and tracking food intake as a means of getting my weight back to a normal range.

From that day forward, I spent every day for the next forty years of my life focused on food and weight in some way or other. I remember my first episode of binge eating at the age of six and how I intuitively knew I had done something wrong that needed to remain secret. There began a forty-year cycle of binging, restricting, dieting, over-exercising, socially isolating from others, and relentlessly obsessing with food, body image, and weight. There began a tormented love-hate relationship with food. There began my life in active food addiction.

My food addiction wasn't just about what I ate—it was about my state of mind. What I weighed and what I ate determined my mood. If I was adhering to a diet or restricting and losing weight, I felt powerful and proud. If I ate "off plan," missed a workout, or was up in weight, I felt guilty, shameful, and weak. But no matter what I ate and no matter what I weighed, one thing never changed. I always lacked peace of mind. I always felt an underlying sense that I was different and somehow defective. Not a day went by that I didn't feel at least one of the following emotions: defeated, disgusted, guilty, sad, angry, punished, less-than, rebellious, determined, shameful, hopeless, helpless, scared, depressed, deprived, or self-conscious. All because I couldn't consistently control my food intake and weight.

In the months before I met Sandra, my life was small. It was reduced to nothing but food and work. I was in so much emotional pain; I wanted to have a normal life, but the overriding urge was to isolate. I stopped participating in social events and had even isolated from my closest friends and family. Physically, my weight had peaked, and I was experiencing debilitating joint pain and fatigue. After years of being a "successful dieter," I had lost the ability to control or moderate certain foods. Perhaps worst of all, food no longer gave me pleasure, yet I kept eating, trying to catch the blissful feelings I used to get from food. I remember feeling utterly hopeless. There was nowhere left to turn.

Then for the first time ever, in late 2017, I heard about food addiction. Instantly, I knew this was what I had been living with and struggling to find peace with for my entire life. I registered for food addiction treatment, and there, I met Sandra.

At the time, I had no idea what impact Sandra would have on me and the course of my life. Somehow, Sandra helped me before my counseling even began. From the moment Sandra walked into the room, I felt comforted and welcomed by her. Sandra immediately shared that she too was a food addict, and that was the precise moment I remember first feeling hope. I felt hope because I could see that Sandra exemplified the one thing I wanted, a peaceful, loving state of being.

Over the next four weeks, Sandra's counseling helped me to identify the thoughts, feelings, and behaviors that kept me in active addiction, and then she provided me with the tools to begin and maintain my recovery. Today, almost five years later, I still use those same tools.

The first tool is a meal plan. I follow a meal plan that is free of my trigger foods, and I commit my daily meal plan to a food sponsor. Having a sponsor is related to the third tool, which I refer to as "community." For me, community means a support system separate from the love and support I get from my friends and family. Community includes others who understand the disease of food addiction because they too have lived with it. Community means always having a connection to someone who "gets it." Community is where support is freely reciprocated among those who understand the disease and risks of relapse.

The second tool I use daily is a spiritual practice. Spiritual practice for me means that I take the time to become present with myself, to avoid overwhelming feelings, to honor my limits, and to consciously try to be the best possible version of myself. If I am in active food addiction, I simply do not have the mental capacity to be fully present with anything or anyone else. Within this personal spiritual practice, I keep in mind the one thing I remember most from Sandra's counseling. She always said that healing comes from a place of love, and she encouraged me to take that approach in all that I do, especially towards myself. That information was life-changing for me.

My life today looks like nothing I could have imagined. I have made peace with both food and my body. I no longer obsess about either. My relationship with food is positive. It's boundaried in a way that gives me mental peace and also allows me to enjoy a meal without the meal being the only focus of the ritual.

I do not experience cravings or feelings of deprivation or hunger anymore. I no longer binge eat or restrict. I no longer over-exercise, pushing my body beyond a reasonable edge. Today, I enjoy moving my body with intention and in connection with what feels good in my soul (for example, walks in nature, dance, and yoga). I stopped using food to try and find fulfillment, and as a result, I discovered what true fulfillment feels like. Today, my life is happy, connected, and peaceful. I have an active social life and no longer isolate due to shame or feeling "less than."

Sandra's counseling not only impacted the course of my personal life but also my career. After over twenty years as a professional pastry chef, I was inspired by Sandra to become a food addiction counselor. I have since completed my training and am currently working with other food addicts, guiding and supporting them in their recovery. As part of this career, I teach cooking classes that support an entirely sugar-free and flour-free lifestyle.

I've been alive for nearly fifty-one years, but I can honestly say that only since entering recovery, have I truly been living.

CHAPTER FOUR

IS YOUR THINKING A FRIEND OR FOE?

> **"**You may believe that you are responsible for what you do, but not for what you think. The truth is that you are responsible for what you think, because it is only at this level that you can exercise choice. What you DO comes from what you think."
>
> – A COURSE IN MIRACLES

I was a prisoner of my mind. So much of my mental real estate was occupied by thoughts of using food. I saw everything that was wrong about me and my life. I thought if I could just stop compulsively overeating and lose weight, everything would be fine. Little did I know, every area of my life had to change.

Today, I know it is absurd to believe that the answer lies in finding the perfect diet and being thin. I was living a life so misaligned from my purpose and so disconnected from my spirit. I needed to examine my entire life. Every area needed healing: how I related to myself, what I believed to be true about myself, how I showed up in all my relationships. My self-hatred and self-condemnation were reflected back to me in every situation I faced, the places I went, and the people I attracted into my life.

Pillar Two: Develop Spirituality and Mindfulness

Addictive eating is mindless eating, and a strong antidote is mindfulness. *One of the obstacles to weight-loss could be your thinking*. Your thoughts can tell you that you're hungry when you're not, and your thinking can convince you that you're a failure when, in fact, the diets were NEVER going to work. They don't work for about ninety-five percent of people. Your mind can decide that exercising today is a bad idea, even though you may have plenty of experience that proves otherwise.

This is where mindfulness comes in. Through spirituality and meditation, we can begin to separate ourselves from our thinking. We can become observers of our thoughts. We are the only species on earth that can think about *what we think about*. A thought is not a command. Nothing in nature is permanent, including a thought, urge, or craving. Everything in nature rises, peaks, and then falls away. At the peak is where most of us act. The peak is when the urge or craving is at its strongest and hardest to resist. The real growth comes when we do not react to the wave of craving but rather let it wash over and away from us.

Spirituality is about tapping into your authentic self, where compulsion doesn't live—a place where you don't experience fear or rage, but rather a place of inner peace, power, and magnificence. You can access this place in your stillness and breath—this is where your power lives.

Often when you've struggled with your weight or eating for years, and maybe even decades, it affects your self-worth. Spirituality is the healing balm; it is a remembering of who you are at your core. We were all born with the spark of the

Divine, an inner strength and wisdom. It's still part of you today. You may just have lost your connection to it.

Bring Meditation Into Your Life

Humans have been benefiting from the practice of meditation for centuries. Think of meditation as medication. I define meditation as connecting to your Spirit—your True Self. It requires us to accept our worthiness and recognize the magnificence with which each of us was born. In a world where most look outside of themselves for validation, comfort, and guidance, spirituality fosters them internally.

There is no wrong way to meditate. It requires no special equipment or trainer and can be practiced anywhere at any given moment. The question you should ask yourself is, "Why am I not mediating yet?"

If meditation is new to you, set realistic expectations for your practice. I started meditating about twenty years ago, and all I could muster was about five to ten *seconds*. Meditation is a practice and a journey. Today, I meditate for sixty minutes most days.

Humanity is hungry for spirituality today. There is a desire and curiosity for a deeper understanding of how we are connected to each other and the earth. There is pull to lead a deeply meaningful life, a sincere desire to feel fully alive. Many high-performing individuals who have achieved status, career success, and money are left wondering, "Is this all there is?" This emptiness results from dismissing the spiritual dimension of our Self.

Meditation will help you develop a rock solid understanding of your worth, your beauty, and your strength. No longer will you be driven to seek validation from people, situations, and successes. Once you solidify this firm understanding, no one needs to give it to you, and no one can take it away from you. You've stepped into your power and magnificence.

Hopefully this has convinced you to begin meditating. I've got nine steps I want to share to set you up for transformation.

1. Posture
   You may not have heard this before, but your posture is important when you meditate. I suggest picking a posture that is relaxed yet alert. If you are able, sit crossed-legged with your chin tucked in. Otherwise, rest comfortably with your legs and arms uncrossed. Close your eyes if you are comfortable doing so. I like to hold a rose quartz crystal, which is known as a healing crystal and the stone of love.

2. Breathing
   The quickest way to quiet a noisy mind is to observe how you are breathing. Feel all the sensations of breath coming in and going out. Monitoring your breathing is a crucial part of meditation, and doing so actually gives your mind something to focus on and helps silence your thoughts. Close your eyes for a moment and affirm that everything is fine, that all is well, and that you are safe. Feel the energy of that mantra.

3. Sound
   Silence can be healing. If you have an anxious mind, silence may be difficult for you, and that is perfectly okay. Remember, there's no wrong way to meditate. An anxious mind may prefer a guided meditation or a moving/talking meditation. This is your quality time with yourself, so do what works for you.

4. Patience

I often hear people say, "I gave meditation a shot, and it didn't really work." Be gentle with yourself. If you experience a fire storm of thoughts, that's a really good meditation session because you've become aware of the storm and how you need not engage with it. The key is to remember this: Meditation is a practice. It's something you'll practice for the rest of your life. In fact, no one masters the art of meditation. However, the more you do it, the more benefits you can gain from it, so it's important to keep going and stick with it. It may be hard at first, but just know that every session brings you closer to a place of peace, self-love, and awareness.

5. Time

If you're new to meditation, I recommend you start with just five minutes a day. Whenever I meditate, I set a timer, put it aside, and then forget about it until it goes off. Over time, you will come to see a significant difference in yourself on the days you don't take time to meditate. Eventually, you will find that five minutes won't be enough. This is a journey with no destination.

6. Location

Think about setting up a meditation area in your home. For some, that might simply be a meditation pillow you pull out from under the bed, a comfy chair by a window, or if you're lucky enough, a room all to yourself. I have a tray where I keep my journal, meditation book, crystals, and a photo of me as a child. You may want to include a vision board where you can focus on how you want your life to unfold. This area will take on a special energy; it will become inviting, and you'll train your brain to know this special area is a place of rejuvenation.

7. Focus

I learned about "equanimity" at a ten-day silent retreat in 2010. The definition of equanimity is a state of psychological stability and composure undisturbed by experience or exposure to emotions, pain, or any other phenomenon that may cause others to lose their emotional balance. Equanimity is a mental calmness, composure, and evenness of temper, especially in a difficult situation. So no matter what storm brews or what other people do, can I be calm in the storm? Can I choose not to react until I have space and time to connect with my inner wisdom? Our recovery cannot depend on the people in our lives behaving well.

8. Intention
    What do you want to bring to the people you will encounter throughout your day, and how can you align your actions with the greater good? You can ask for guidance during your meditation time. I always have a pen handy to take down my inspirations and allow ideas to flow through me to the page. Once you have taken the time to fill up your spiritual tank, you will have more to give and a greater capacity to receive.
    Feel free to use this intention: **I want to be an expression of love and vibrate at a high frequency so high that others raise up with me.**
    Doing this, you'll be surprised how everyone you meet will rise up to meet you at this vibration. Setting an intention for your meditation, and even setting an intention for your day, will impact the day itself and show you just how powerful you can be when you're connected to yourself and your spirit.

9. Enjoyment
    Lastly, I want meditation to be something you enjoy. It should never feel like a chore, and one great way to ensure it never does is to shut your eyes and smile as you meditate. Feel the energy of that. Your brain will know you're smiling, and you'll feel great.

Meditation can drastically impact how you approach life, how personally you take things, and even how you interact with others. Meditation teaches you to release the need to react to situations immediately and instead take time and space to respond with grace. Meditation can enhance your compassion and allow you to see things more clearly, including yourself, giving you a sense of calmness and centeredness. It helped me learn to love myself unconditionally and achieve peace with myself, which allowed me to also find peace with others. And this is what I believe meditation can do for you too.

Are Your Thoughts Draining or Energizing You?

Your thoughts are powerful. Your thoughts drive action and produce emotions. You are in the driver's seat of your thinking—each moment you get to decide what you will focus on.

Let's explore the power of the mind and how this power relates to trigger foods and addiction. Young minds are like sponges, open and able to absorb everything around them. Through the repetition and practice of thinking, acting, and feeling, neural pathways grow stronger and transform into habits.

At what age did you start to associate food with comfort, love, and escape? How many times have self-deprecating thoughts and crippling feelings made you turn to eating for comfort? Developing a new neural pathway or habit is similar to stepping into a field of untouched snow, and forging a path through the snow is hard. But each time you walk that same path, it becomes easier. So each time we eat for comfort, we reinforce a neural pathway until this behavior feels almost automatic.

Tape Reel: The Burden of Loneliness, OCTOBER 1980

Loneliness is a big trigger for me, even up to the present day. I experienced profound loneliness as a child.

I am sitting in the basement, crying because I'm not allowed to go out for Halloween. My older sister is trying to comfort me by reminding me that it will be my eighth birthday tomorrow. I literally had no idea. Up until this point, my birthday has never been acknowledged—I never got a cake with candles or gifts. Everyone in my home is just trying to survive, and I feel like I don't have a place in it.

I miss thirty to forty days of school each year, not because I want to, but because my mom preferred I didn't go. Things were easier for her when I stayed home. It eased her worry. On the days that I would go, loneliness followed me. My attendance has been so poor that I struggle to make friends, and so, my social interaction with other children is limited. My summer break was spent at home, not far from my mom, seeing very little of the outside world on those beautiful summer days. I'm filled with a sadness that I am not yet capable of processing.

Currently, on Friday nights when my daughter is with her dad, and I don't have plans, that same profound loneliness washes over me. At these times, food becomes very loud for me. In the past, a lonely Friday or Sunday night would involve compulsive overeating to the point of complete numbness. Then I'd flip over to hating myself for failing to identify what triggered me—I could never deal with loneliness.

Today, I've learned that I'm as lonely as I decide to be. I make plans earlier in the week so I have people I can enjoy spending time with on the weekend. And I'm okay being alone, even if it means I grieve or feel uncomfortable feelings. Uncomfortable feelings don't scare me as much anymore. Meditation has shown me that I can feel, observe, and release all feelings that do not serve me.

Trigger, Thought, Action

Let me break down the components of using food for comfort:

1. **Trigger** – An emotion, a situation, a person, a place, a memory.
2. **Thought** – i.e. "I want comfort. I want to numb-out with food." Sometimes the addictive eating is so automatic we don't recognize or hear the thought before we begin to eat compulsively.
3. **Action** – Compulsive eating, relief, comfort, numbness.

Each time I dance these three steps—get triggered, eat, feel comfort—I strengthen my neural pathway until this dance becomes automatic. It is no different than hitting the brakes each time I see a red light.

Even though I was desperate to stop cycling through the same three, damaging steps over and over again, I was unable to gain control. As a result, I continued to eat.

Your Mind: Friend or Foe?

Looking back, as a young adult, I was clearly unable to trust my thinking when it came to food. I could not objectively perceive my world.

What do I mean by that? I mean that I had developed neural pathways that told me to eat when I was scared, sad, and lonely. Over time, many of my life's problems were subdued by eating. But they were never resolved. And then celebrating and socializing meant eating—all roads led to eating. But ultimately I used food to numb-out. Sadly, I could not just numb the bad feelings. I numbed all feelings, including joy and happiness.

Then in my thirties, not only was I a food addict, I felt unfit for this life. I had not learned how to handle life's disappointments or grow as a person through difficult times. Instead, anytime I was faced with something unmanageable, I drew the blinds, I hid, and I ate. I stopped maturing emotionally.

Over time, my mind turned on me. It told me I was stupid, fat, and unlovable.

We all have mental tapes that play in the background, sort of like the soundtrack to our lives. Emotional events will often trigger these mental tapes. Typical triggers include failure in all its forms, whether it be a mistake, a bad grade, or a romantic rejection. We all have our "go to" mental tapes. Do you ever stop and take a good listen?

My mental tape played the most discouraging, hopeless tune I could possibly sing to myself. Caring for my bipolar mother often triggered it. It went like this: "My life is horrible. It is never going to get better. It is only going to get worse." This would loop over and over in my mind. I would play this tape when I was most upset.

If you repeat something long enough, with enough emotional intensity, you will believe it. And once it becomes a belief, it manifests in your life. I did a great job of it! I *thought my way* to becoming a twenty-nine-year-old living with morbid obesity, unable to work, on a cocktail of antidepressants and mood stabilizers. I *thought my way* to becoming a twenty-nine-year-old who could Not. Take. Another. Step. I wanted to die.

My wish for death just made sense. With thoughts like, "My life is horrible. It is never going to get better. It's only going to get worse," playing on repeat, anyone would have trouble getting out of bed.

So I had to come up with a new mental tape that I could play instead, one with great, positive emotional intensity. Whenever my old tape started playing, I would hit the figurative stop button and replace those negative thoughts with a new mental tape: "My life is filled with blessings and miracles. My life is filled with blessings and miracles. My life is filled with blessings and miracles." I played this tape when sadness and darkness descended. At first, I didn't believe this mental tape, but I knew I had to play it with the same emotional intensity and for the same length of time as I had played my previous, destructive tape. If I think back, I didn't believe the destructive tape when I first started rehearsing it in my mind, but with enough practice, it manifested itself in my life. The same had to be true for my new tape—*I just had to practice it.*

Food addiction and obesity robbed me of a mom. Diabetes ravaged her body. She had nerve damage to her knees and could not walk unassisted. Her eyesight was failing, she had lost all her teeth, and she was incontinent. I remember visiting a very busy Yorkdale Mall in Toronto with my mother. She had soiled her pants. That day, I started to retrain my brain. I held my head high, pulled my shoulders back, and proudly walked my mom to the bathroom as I repeated, "My life is filled with blessings and miracles. My life is filled with blessings and miracles." I played my new mental tape often and with great intensity, and it manifested in my life.

This is when real change happens, when you believe in something you cannot yet see. Create a new mental tape that will inspire you. As you consider how to weaken and rewire the toxic neural pathways in your life, start by identifying your triggers. Does loneliness lead to eating? This awareness will give you a chance to overcome that trigger. Next time you are about to "use" food, PAUSE. In the silence of a pause, *grace* can enter. Pause gives you just enough time and space to reach for a tool or life line. Know ahead of time which tool serves you best. Is it breathing? Walking? Drinking water? Making a phone call? Connecting with people? Praying?

Remember that cravings are almost always lies—the lie of "just one bite," "you deserve a treat today," or "the diet will start tomorrow."

Each time you choose differently, your old neural pathway weakens. Every time you "lay new tracks in the snow," it gets easier to follow the right path.

Can You Think on Purpose?

Your energy level is an excellent barometer on your thinking. High-quality thinking leads to feeling energized, hopeful, and motivated. Low-quality thinking leads to feeling depleted, hopeless, and unmotivated.

Let's say you slipped and ate in a way that made you unhappy. Low-quality thinking would sound like, "What's wrong with me?" or "Now I've blown it, so I'm really going to town" or "Trying to lose weight is never going to work for me."

Low-quality thinking will inflict pain, and you're the abuser in this case. One of the biggest drives for "using" food is pain relief. The good news is that because you're the one causing the pain, you can put a stop to it.

High-quality thinking would sound like, "That meal was a moment in time gone forever. There's nothing I can do to bring it back" or "I'm human. I'm not perfect. I can't speak perfectly, act perfectly, or eat perfectly" or "The slip was a call for love, and I can give myself that love." High-quality thinking leads to higher-quality actions. The quickest way to get back on the wagon is through kindness and compassion. Let go of the past so you can live this moment to the fullest.

Next time you have a slip with your eating, DO NOT call it a mistake. Reframe it as a call for love.

Body, Mind, Spirit

Let me take you through my recovery through the lens of body, mind, and spirit.

Body

My body needs proper nutrition, and it needs to move each day—simple to say, but harder to do! *I did not have another diet in me.* I already knew what to eat and what *not* to eat. Lack of knowledge had never been the problem. I was always searching for the perfect diet, and I know now it does not exist. So I took a simple approach and eliminated—to the best of my ability—trigger foods that would inevitably set off a compulsive overeating episode. I knew if I could stop overeating, I could be healthy.

Exercise began from a humble place. I had to become willing *to be willing* to exercise. I was twenty-nine years old and weighed over 260 pounds, so all I could do was walk fifteen minutes at a time. I was so embarrassed that my peers could exercise so much more than me. I turned things around when I became grateful that I could walk for fifteen minutes. Powered by positivity, I focused on increasing this time, and it did expand. Slowly, that fifteen-minute walk turned into thirty minutes. Then that walk progressed into a jog, which turned into a five-kilometer run, which grew to ten kilometers, and finally, a half marathon!

Mind

I had a physical craving for sugar, flour, and fat. I obsessed about where to get my trigger foods, how much to have, and when I could eat them, only stopping when I became too physically sick to eat any more. As it is with drugs and alcohol, the only way to eliminate cravings is to eliminate the drug. For me, it was refined sugar and refined flour, and as the drug left my system, so did the cravings.

I had to radically reconsider how I viewed certain foods and accept that sugar and flour are poison in my body, slowly robbing me of my life, with the potential to eventually kill me. I changed my mental tapes that told me I was undisciplined, lazy, and ugly. I retrained my mind to see the beauty in me, to love and accept myself exactly where I was *before* losing weight.

Spirit

I really believe I was a compulsive overeater because my life was so misaligned with my life's purpose, and the pain that caused led me to use food. I had to trust in something other than food for comfort, and that was faith. I take time each day to meditate, to become quiet and still, and to tap into my intuition.

Intuition is the great equalizer. Rich or poor, educated or uneducated, young or old—we are all born with an inner wisdom far superior to our intellect, and the quieter we are, the louder our inner voice becomes. The more we follow our intuition, the stronger it becomes. This inner wisdom is my guide when selecting food, understanding when I am full, and recognizing my worth and beauty, which allows me to be at peace with food, myself, and those around me.

This process of self-knowledge and acceptance was epitomized by my throwing my scale in the trash. I released myself from the bondage of the scale. That number does not define me anymore. It is no longer the prize I strive for. Instead, the prize I win for living well is feeling great. My body isn't perfect, but I am perfectly in love with myself. My job has been an ongoing, daily commitment to abstaining from my trigger foods, taking time to connect to my spirit, and understanding that my thoughts are powerful.

What you feed your mind is infinitely more important than what you put into your mouth.

Nothing will slow you down more than discouragement. What are the first thoughts you have in the morning? How do those thoughts affect the rest of your day? In my twenties, I would often wake to negative thoughts invading my mind: "I really hate myself. I really hate how I ate yesterday. I really hate my body." These thoughts would affect my feelings. I would feel hopeless, drained, and depressed. These emotions would affect my energy. I felt depleted, uninspired, joyless, and pessimistic. This was a painful state of existence, and food offered comfort. I was causing myself pain, and I was looking for pain relief in my trigger foods.

The thoughts you allow to occupy your mind will affect your motivation and energy. Start building energy, momentum, and inspiration in your life. Start your day by looking for everything that is right and beautiful about you! Practice unconditional acceptance of yourself *as you are today.* Love yourself now just as you'll love yourself when you lose weight—that is unconditional, unchanging love! This kind of thinking will affect how you feel—it will bring hope, encouragement, and energy. This new energy will bring inspiration. You will feel more in the flow. You'll attract new ideas, new ways of moving forward. You'll be in a high vibrational state where more is available to you. From this place, you are more capable of caring and nurturing your body, mind, and spirit. Everything begins with a thought—choose wisely. Choose with love.

High-quality thinking leads to high-quality decision-making, creating a high-quality life.

Smash the diet mentality and emerge a new person. Stop fighting food, stop fearing food, stop trying to control food. Move away from words like, "I must" and "I shouldn't," and start selecting food from your inner knowing, a place of peace. Release the perfectionism that comes with dieting and the media's expectations of beauty. In moments of uncertainty, tell yourself this: ***I'm not perfect. My body isn't perfect, but I'm perfectly in love with myself.***

There's no more starting over. There's no more "the diet starts tomorrow" or feeling shame about mistakes made. Instead, there's this beautiful realization that you are exactly where you need to be, and the better you live in this moment, the better the next moment will be.

Ultimately, I was able to achieve food serenity by taking my eyes off the ball of dieting and turning them inward, towards the way I was thinking about myself and the life I was leading. If I could go back in time to when I started that new fancy job, I would tell myself that I didn't need a fancy dietician. I needed only to focus on self-love.

The day I took my eyes off the scale was the day I found freedom. I was able to let go of the business of dieting and perfectionism and invest in the business of eating whole, fresh foods, moving my body, and giving myself unconditional love, no matter what my weight ended up being.

My weight is none of my business! I did, and still do, the work of recovery, and I let God take care of my weight.

Wherever your weight ends up, it ends up. You cannot control the number on the scale, but you can control your behaviors and perspectives. When your behaviors fall short, focus on your perspective. Appreciate what's gone well and encourage yourself to keep going.

Today, I understand the power of my mind. Everything starts with a thought—thoughts produce emotions, and words influence actions.

66 Your beliefs become your thoughts.
Your thoughts become your words.
Your words become your actions.
Your actions become your habits.
Your habits become your values.
Your values become your destiny."

– MANTMA GANDHI

In this chapter, we explored how developing a spirituality and mindfulness practice can help you cultivate the self-love necessary to overcome food addiction. Next, we will look at the final pillar and address the importance of establishing a support network that will catch you when you falter during your journey towards food serenity.

Chapter Four Exercises

Exercise #1: Create Your Own Mantra

Retrain your brain. Give your subconscious mind instructions for creating the body, health, and life of your dreams. Take a moment to write a mantra for yourself. It should be simple and positive. Here are some examples:

"I look at life through the eyes of love. I can see all that is right and beautiful about me."

"I was born with the spark of the Divine. This flame of magnificence burns bright inside of me."

"I invite the Divine to guide my thinking, my actions, and my words today."

"My life is filled with blessings and miracles."

_____

_____

_____

_____

_____

Say this mantra with intensity and often! Every time you get up to go to the washroom, walk to your car, or pour a glass of water, press play on your mantra.

Exercise #2: Reframe Your Monologue After a Slip with Food

Think back to your last compulsive eating episode. What was happening at the time? Can you imagine showing yourself compassionate curiosity during that time? Were you calling for love? Journal here about your call for love:

_____

_____

_____

_____

_____

Exercise #3: Begin the Journey to Meditation

There is no wrong way to meditate. You will never master meditation, and every session is a chance to know yourself better. You are a physical, mental, and spiritual being. Each of these areas needs time, attention, and care. Take time to research three different approaches or practices to meditation. Record your research findings here:

_____

_____

_____

_____

_____

Meet Annelise

I spent most of my life dieting and have tried every single diet on the market more than once. My very first diet started when I was ten years old. I became an expert dieter, but the diets never worked for me. I always did well for a short period of time, and then, inevitably, in four to six months, after losing significant weight, I would buy into the diet industry's mantra of moderation. Before I knew it, I would begin eating uncontrollably and gaining weight again.

Before I took Sandra's program, this is how the last thirty years of my life looked. I constantly felt like a failure because, somehow, everyone else could figure out weight-loss but me. I kept searching for the magic answer that would make healthy living all manageable. My relationship with food was hateful and abusive. I was either dieting, eating very little food and feeling deprived, or I was revolting against the diets and the constant feelings of worthlessness that arose from eating everything in sight, mostly highly processed foods with very little nutrition but lots of salt, fat, and sugar.

Sandra opened my eyes to food addiction and helped me understand that everyone else doesn't just figure out weight-loss. There are many people who struggle with food addiction, just like me. Learning to see my abuse of food through the lens of addiction filled in that missing piece of the puzzle I never had. Now I also carry a whole toolbox of resources that help me navigate food sobriety—and they actually make sense of everything circling around in my head about food.

Armed with a better understanding of my addiction and how it impacts my thinking, I am now learning to build a daily routine that combats the lies I tell myself about food. I start the day with meditation to quiet and center my mind, then I repeat affirmations to help build my self-efficacy. I follow a structured meal plan because it's not safe for me to "wing it" with food. Most importantly, with Sandra's help, I have come to fully understand that I cannot eat my trigger foods. Moderation doesn't work for me, and it's okay to eliminate these processed, calorically dense, high-fat, salty, and sugary foods because they are not real, whole foods and don't need to be moderated. For me, abstinence is the only solution because it is far too difficult to moderate my consumption of these foods. I believe I can find the food serenity I am looking for by eliminating my trigger foods.

I am still near the beginning of my journey to food serenity, but since starting Sandra's program, my eyes have opened and are seeing clearly for the first time that I am a food addict. Acknowledging this frees me from feeling like an inadequate failure. I can be happy now. I can love myself as I am. And I can use the tools from Sandra's program to get me to where I want to be, knowing that I will eventually arrive there—not by seeing how little I can eat until I just can't take it, but by being mindful of what is happening in those moments where I want my trigger foods, turning to the tools, and reaching out for help.

Right now, I lean heavily on morning meditation to set my intentions for the day. I then take each day just one meal at a time. As I embark on my journey of abstinence from my trigger foods to finally achieve a peaceful relationship with food, I know a long road lies ahead. I will not walk it perfectly, but if I stay the course and love myself throughout, I will get there, having enjoyed the journey.

CHAPTER FIVE

FINDING YOUR PEOPLE

66 We are going to know a new
freedom and a new happiness.
We will not regret the past nor
wish to shut the door on it.
We will comprehend the word
'serenity' and we will know peace.
No matter how far down the
scale we have gone, we will see how
our experience can benefit others."

– BIG BOOK OF ALCOHOLICS ANONYMOUS

Tape Reel: Turning Point, OCTOBER 2001

"Mail this letter." These were the last words my husband spoke as he left for work, and I replied hastily as the door closed behind him, "Okay."

This simple request was the only thing that was required of me that day, but it immediately felt like an impossible task. I stared at the letter, trying to will my husband to return so I could give it back to him and tell him I couldn't do it. But the sound of the car engine had already died away in the distance. I sighed and slumped further into the sofa.

I was exhausted and frustrated. Depression had overtaken my life, and I was one month into my extended sick leave. Nothing felt manageable. The years of struggle with both my weight and eating had been detrimental. I was done. I needed a way out.

I had no idea what guided me to the shelf above the stove or what I was looking for. And I certainly had no idea that my life was about to completely change. But I found myself reaching for the hefty copy of the White Pages directory and flipping the book open to the phone number for Overeaters Anonymous (OA), which offered a twelve-step program. I dialed the number, and a soothing male voice responded. Mark, who had used his home number in the listing, kindly invited me to a meeting in Toronto's North York area.

How hard it must have been for him to deal with someone like me: so broken, hopeless, and helpless. I imagined his life as serene and perfect. I truly had no idea what he had been through. "I'll look for you tonight," he said, and I felt the faintest sense of hope. Maybe this OA thing could work for me…

I arrived at the meeting early and sat in my car while I coaxed out the courage to go inside. Mark greeted me at the entrance to the church basement. I scanned the room and saw there were about twenty people present, all of us women except for Mark.

He introduced me to the group and made me feel immediately welcome. I chose a seat in the back, not knowing what to expect. I was surprised that everyone looked "normal."

After some preamble, Susie stood up and read "How it Works" from The Big Book of Alcoholics Anonymous: "Without help, it is too much for us. But here is One who has all power—that One is God. May you find Her now! Half measures availed us nothing. We stood at the turning point. We asked Her protection and care with complete abandon." As I listened, I realized…they get it! They understand me! My hope deepened. I wasn't alone. Here was a group of people who had experienced the same struggles and come out the other side. If they could do it, maybe I could too.

I took a breath and realized I belonged here. These were my people. This was my beginning. At this moment, the search for the perfect diet was over. I began to treat my eating as an addiction.

<u>Disclaimer</u>: I no longer attend a twelve-step program, but it was, without a doubt, the foundation of my recovery. It worked for me at a time when I could no longer trust my thinking when it came to eating, and I needed to surrender to a program and a power greater than myself. There are many roads to recovery, and a twelve-step program is only one of them. Just know they don't work for everyone.

Let's recap. In chapter three, we discussed the three pillars to recovery from food addiction:

- **Pillar One:** Eliminate Trigger Foods
- **Pillar Two:** Develop Spirituality and Mindfulness
- **Pillar Three:** Belong to a Support Network

We've covered the importance of eliminating addictive foods and developing spirituality and mindfulness. Now I want to dive deeper into the support network pillar.

Pillar Three: Belong to a Support Network

Find Your Community

You will need a support network consisting of people striving to achieve the same goal as you in order to eliminate your trigger foods. Find a place that is inclusive, safe, and welcoming. Find a place where you can learn to listen to that intuitive voice that wants you to love yourself unconditionally and lead a life full of meaning. And if you can't find that network near you right now, you're welcome to join me in my Food Addiction Recovery Program and make friendships with other people like us, who want to fundamentally change their relationship with food, at sandraelia.com.

As you read this chapter, I want you to feel that you've unlocked a safe, sacred space where you find the courage to seek the truth about yourself, to see the beauty that has always been present, and to transform your vulnerabilities into power.

Throughout this book, I have striven to lead by example and be as vulnerable as possible. I've worked hard to break through the barriers of food addiction and present a plan that can actually work for you. I am sharing my truths and stories to inspire you to create a support network that will walk alongside you on your Food Addiction Recovery Journey.

Overeaters Anonymous has something called Dignity of Choice, which means you define your own meal plan—whatever works for you. By contrast, other anonymous programs will often give you a very prescribed meal plan that you should follow in order to remain in recovery. Some people need a tremendous amount of support and structure while other people need more freedom to choose for themselves. Depending on the kind of person you are and what works for you, you may be pulled to one program more than another, and that is completely okay.

The One Caveat

Now, there is one caveat to twelve-step meetings that I feel I must share with you. Let's say you're thinking about joining a twelve-step program, but you're unsure. Well, you need to attend *at least* six meetings before you make your final decision.

And this is really, really important.

Most people go to one meeting, think to themselves, "This is too weird. I'm not doing this. This is crazy. The steps sound too hard. No, not doing this." But here's the thing: You can't fully see and understand everything a twelve-step program can offer by attending just one meeting. Instead, you need to make a commitment and see if, after six meetings, you're still hearing the same dialogue in your brain.

It's important to understand that every meeting has its own flavor depending on the members in attendance and their energies. So if you happen to come across a meeting that doesn't really feel like a good fit for you, know that's okay, and try a different meeting. But give twelve-step program meetings at least six tries.

And remember: No contempt prior to examination.

Again, my goal is not to push a twelve-step program onto you. What I am trying to convey is the possibility of reaching a turning point in one. I'm showing you what the twelve-step program could do for you, especially if you're struggling to find a community of support, which is the third pillar. Trust me. This is the easiest support network you can tap into.

The Twelve Steps to Recovery

Before we dive into the twelve steps, there is something I do feel needs to be addressed, and that is the *God issue*. Almost every step within the twelve steps uses the word "God." Now, what I want you to understand is that the program makes it very, *very* clear that the "God" mentioned is a god of your own understanding and your own definition.

Religion is never discussed in these twelve-step programs because the programs are meant to be available and accessible to everyone across the world. So please understand that, given twelve-step programs were written in the 1930's, when the steps say "God," it is only because it was the most common Western term for religious deities at the time.

With that said, if the word "God" is still causing you distress as you consider whether to embark on a twelve-step program, know that the program encourages people to replace "God" with "Higher Power," "Buddha," "nature," or any other being or thing that makes them feel comfortable.

I'm going to pull back the curtain, share my shorthand notes, and help you understand how you can apply the steps to your journey.

Step #1: We admitted we were powerless over alcohol [trigger foods]—that our lives had become unmanageable.

While this is only the first step, this is also where a lot of people look for the exit sign when attending their first twelve-step meeting. Oftentimes, people don't want to admit powerlessness over certain foods and don't feel their lives have become unmanageable. These people will often think to themselves, "What are you talking about? My life is manageable. I have a job. I have a family. I pay the bills. There's nothing unmanageable about my life, and I'm not powerless when confronted by a cupcake. Everything in moderation, they say."

Here's my take on this. There *is* a powerlessness to being stuck in an addiction loop. Craving and wanting lead to compulsive overeating. Once the overeating episode is done, we are often filled with remorse, guilt, and shame. We feel so bad that we are desperate to stop "using" food. We stop for a short time, only to experience the pain of physical and psychological withdrawal from our trigger foods, causing us to "use" food again.

Round and round we have gone for years, maybe even decades. Each time I eat a trigger food, something happens to my brain and body that is almost impossible to control. In other words, what happens is the phenomenon of craving and obsession. This hasn't happened just a few times. I have evidence of it happening thousands of times in my past. I'm safer when I don't have my trigger foods.

Sure, I was paying my bills, and I had a steady job, but the enormous mental real estate occupied by thoughts like, "What am I going to eat? When am I going to eat? How much am I going to eat? Did I eat too little? Can I have some more? Did I eat too much? Should I even eat dinner?" was unmanageable. The perpetual mental chatter was almost too much for anyone to handle. It was definitely too much for me, and if this is something you feel you relate to, then I suggest you take the first step by admitting it to yourself.

My next step was cutting out my trigger foods. It was too difficult to tackle the areas of my life that drove me to eat for comfort while I continued using food as a coping mechanism. I needed to eliminate that crutch and eat solely for nourishment.

I relapsed multiple times during my first year and a half at Overeaters Anonymous. I would get through seven days and then relapse. Then reach fourteen days and relapse. Then reach sixty days and relapse. I saw each relapse as failure. I didn't have the wisdom or perspective to understand that I was, in fact, making progress.

What I know today is that the belief that I was failing actually slowed down my progress. As they say in the program, "Progress over perfection."

My motivation increased as I listened to others share their struggles with eating and weight in depth. I found strength listening to women who had experienced a strong recovery but struggled with defects of character, just like me. I heard stories of women who had endured much worse than me but still had the courage to face their demons head-on. That's when I knew I could do it too.

Step #2: We came to believe that a Power greater than ourselves could restore us to sanity.

> "Lack of power, that was our dilemma. We had to find a power by which we could live, and it had to be a Power greater than ourselves. Obviously. But where and how were we to find this power? Well, that's exactly what this book is about. Its main object is to enable you to find a power greater than yourself which will solve your problem."
>
> – BIG BOOK OF ALCOHOLICS ANONYMOUS

I've read the *Big Book of Alcoholics Anonymous* over five times, always replacing the word "alcohol" with "trigger food," but it wasn't until the last read-through that I discovered its main object. You would think the main object of a book called *Alcoholics Anonymous* would be encouraging readers to stop "using" alcohol, but that's not it. The main object is this: "Find a Power greater than yourself which will solve your problem."

My addiction had completely decimated my life. I desperately needed a power beyond myself to guide me through situations that baffled me.

When I started attending twelve-step meetings in old church basements, my faith bucket was empty. All I had was a little prayer I had developed when I was really struggling with food. I would pray, "Okay, God, I'm not going to 'use' food. Now you take care of everything else." I would pray, "Everything else, God, you figure it out. You figure out the anxiety and fear. You figure out how I'm going to tell my aunt that I can't eat her special dessert." Since I felt I couldn't manage any of that, I decided to surrender. I decided to let go as you would when you want to float in water. God could take care of things. I would do my part, and I would have faith that She would do Her part, and every time things worked out, I would put a pebble in my faith bucket.

Over time, that bucket began to overflow—and I'm extremely proud to say that I have unshakeable faith because God helped me in tough times through surrender and pure prayer. Believing in a Higher Power is all about having faith, so lean into your faith when you're overwhelmed with urges and cravings to eat compulsively. Your Higher Power will carry you through cravings.

Step #3: We made a decision to turn our will and our lives over to the care of God as we understood Her.

At the darkest period of my life, I believed God didn't love me, and I was alone. This step is really about your relationship with your God and how you relate to your Higher Power. For me, this was really tricky because I grew up Catholic, and honestly, it's still something I'm recovering from. Growing up, I was told that if I prayed hard enough, and if I earned God's favor, She would answer my prayers. I was only four or five when I first heard this, and at that young age, I became a compulsive prayer. I would pray for the violence and chaos in my house to stop. I would pray to be seen. I really thought that if I said enough Hail Marys and Our Fathers, God would listen. I really thought if I just behaved a little better, I would fall into Her favor. But my prayers were never answered. Instead, the violence and chaos persisted, and I continued to feel unseen and unheard by the people who I thought were supposed to show me the most love and affection.

Because of these experiences, I became an adult with a devastating food addiction. Everyone at the twelve-step program told me that I needed to develop my relationship with God so that She could stop me from compulsively overeating. Of course, I didn't believe it. I would think to myself, "Really? *Now* God is going to help me? Not then, when I was a kid dealing with violence and serious chaos in my life, but *now?* Yeah, right." Then, I entered the mindset that if She helped me with my food addiction *now*, I would be very upset because She didn't help me then, when I felt I needed the most help.

Despite all my doubt in God, in order to recover from food addiction, I had to develop some kind of relationship with a Higher Power in my adult life. I ended up letting go of my old relationship with God, the one taught to me by the church, and instead created my own, healthy relationship where I made the rules of how I would relate to a Higher Power. Actually, I was inspired to do this by a beautiful speaker who discussed her own Higher Power. She said her Higher Power *loved* her, thought she was precious, and gave her everything she needed any time she needed help. She said God would send her armies of angels to protect her. Then at the end of her presentation, she said, "If you want to use my definition of God, feel free," and I did. It was amazing. I was able to reconceptualize my whole idea of God and my whole relationship with God. I made it new. I made it what I needed it to be so that I could free myself from the constraints of the life I was living, so I could become the person I wanted to be and experience the self-love that I needed.

If your relationship with your God was anything like mine, I ask you to please reconceptualize. Understand *Her* in a way that makes you feel seen, heard, and loved. And if you're still struggling, feel free to use my definition:

My God loves and adores me.
God is as accessible as my next breath.
At any time, I can fall into Her arms,
and She will carry me.
God is ready and waiting to
guide me to the next right step.
I'm precious. I'm worthy,
and I'm enough in Her eyes.

Step #4: We made a searching and fearless moral inventory of ourselves.

This is another step that sends a lot of people running for the exit, and here's why. This step in the program asks you to take a light and shine it across your whole life. This step asks you to confront your fears, your resentments, your wrongdoings, your sexual blights—basically, all the gunk and garbage you've carried with you throughout your life.

There's a saying that goes, "You're only as sick as your secrets," and all this step does is ask you to write all those secrets down, categorize, and organize them. Now I know this may be hard. I know this is one of those things we *don't* want to acknowledge. But doing so gives you the gift of recognizing your unhealthy patterns. Through this painful process of self-reflection, you begin to really understand yourself and why you do the things you do.

Step #5: We admitted to God, to ourselves, and to another human being the exact nature of our wrongs.

When I got to this step, I remember thinking to myself, "Yeah, I'll admit this stuff to God, and I'm cool admitting it to myself, but I'm not telling another human being. That would just humiliate me. I already feel bad about myself. Don't make me tell somebody this."

Almost everyone has what twelve-steppers call Grave Takers—things that have happened to you or that you've done that you are never going to share with anyone, things you're going to take to your grave. So I thought, "No way. I'm not going to tell anybody what I've been through."

Eventually I did come around because I knew it was what I had to do to heal. I knew it was what I had to do to begin recovering from my food addiction. Now I always say that God loves me so much that when I finally decided to share my Grave Taker with another human being, it just so happened that she had the exact same Grave Taker.

I remember her looking at me and saying, "Yeah, I did that too," and I just couldn't help but feel wowed by life.

The gift of this step was the realization that I'm no better and no worse than anyone else. Instead, I'm just part of the human race. This step taught me that when I'm able to share the worst parts of me, the biggest mistakes and most awful behavior, I will still be loved and accepted.

Step #6: We were entirely ready to have God remove all these defects of character.

Now this step is very simple, and it all goes back to Step #4: Make A Searching and Fearless Moral Inventory of Yourself.

Once you have pulled back the curtains and seen yourself and your life for what they are, once you have recognized and organized your patterns and defects, it is time to allow God to remove all of these defects.

It is time to start anew and be born again.

It is time to start living the life you want to live and loving yourself for all you are and can be.

Step #7: We humbly asked Him to remove our shortcomings.

Before I describe this step, I want you to note something. The point of these twelve steps is to experience a spiritual awakening. I know that may seem like such an elusive concept. I know you may be telling yourself, like I did, "I want that spiritual awakening! When is it coming?" I yearned for a beautiful spiritual awakening, and it happened for me here, when I reached step #7.

I used to call myself a student of Overeaters Anonymous. That meant I went to three "classes" (meetings) a week, I called my sponsor every day, and I did all my "homework assignments" (steps). Then I got to step #7, and I realized there's no instruction, just "Humbly Ask God to Remove All of Your Shortcomings." I thought, "There's not much here to go with."

But I pushed on, and I wrote them all out—all seventy-nine shortcomings. Then I lit candles and got on my knees, preparing in a very ceremonial way to ask God to remove all of my shortcomings. What came out of my mouth was a complete shock to me: "God, I fucking hate you." At that moment, I remember thinking something terrible was going to happen. God was really going to punish me now. When I confessed my true feelings to God, I felt like I was cracked open and a swoosh of unconditional love from God poured over me. Despite admitting my hatred for God, all I felt from her in that moment was love—pure, unconditional love—and it was so overwhelming that I had to lie in bed and sob in a fetal position. I was overwhelmed by God's love. This was my spiritual awakening.

You never know when your spiritual awakening is going to hit. It can happen at any step.

This is the purpose of twelve-step programs.

Step #8: We made a list of all persons we had harmed and became willing to make amends to them all.

Like step #6, this step is simple. It is just a matter of making a list, whether mentally or with pen and paper, of all the people you know you have harmed. That harm could have been inflicted with your words, your actions, or anything else. Once you have your list, it is up to you to take a deep breath and be willing to right the wrongs you've done to others and make amends to them all—even the ones you believe played a part in your hurtful behavior.

Step #9: We made direct amends to such people wherever possible, except when to do so would injure them or others.

This is another step that intimidates people. It's one thing to make a list of all the people you've harmed and are *willing* to make amends to, but it is something else entirely to actually *make* direct amends. Often the defense response here is, "I'm not apologizing. You don't understand. Sure, I did that to them, but you don't know what they did to me."

A lot of times, when people attend their first or second twelve-step meeting, they look at the twelve steps and think, "I can't do this. This is too much. I'm going to leave." And the truth is, these people are right. We can't do all these steps so early in recovery, and we're not supposed to. Each step is designed to equip you with the strength and perspective necessary to complete the next step. You're not ready to do step #9 when you've just entered your first meeting. You're only ready when you've completed the first eight steps, and that is something that you need to consider before you decide to find the door and leave your very first meeting. Don't worry about all the steps when you haven't completed the first one. Instead, take things step by step. Once you do, you'll see that you may be ready to make amends even if you originally thought it was something you could never do.

A beautiful thing about this program is that it presents you with so much wisdom. When I got to step #9, I was told to create three buckets: one for people I would apologize to immediately, one for the people it would be uncomfortable to apologize to, and one for the people I felt I would never apologize to.

When I got through the first bucket, I felt relieved. I remember thinking, "Oh, that felt nice. That felt good. A weight has been lifted off my shoulders. Okay, I'll try the second bucket." And the second bucket was more difficult, but I got through it and thought to myself, "Wow, that felt amazing." I felt like miracles were starting to happen. I was beginning to look at myself and the world differently, and these feelings actually made tackling the third bucket possible. I was able to make amends with people I thought I would never make amends with, and I felt so strong, like my life was really starting to change. So I want you to know this is possible for you too. Once you get through the first bucket, and then the second, the third will just come naturally. Before you know it, you'll have made amends with all those you felt you never could, and you'll feel lighter and better.

When I "used" food, I felt tremendous pain, so much pain that I couldn't see or bear to admit that I was inflicting pain on the people around me. It was never my intention or plan. Could this be true for those who have hurt me? Could they be in pain? Could this person causing me pain also be sick? Was their sickness upsetting me? Could I forgive them just as I sought forgiveness from others? This is the great lesson of step #9.

The last three steps in the program are really about maintenance, which is crucial to your recovery.

Step #10: We continued to take personal inventory, and when we were wrong, promptly admitted it.

This step is sort of like when you've done a big and thorough house-cleaning. It is now your job to make sure to do daily checkups and sweeps and dustings here and there to make sure the house doesn't get as dirty as it was prior to that first thorough cleaning. Trust me—you don't want to have to make those big, difficult apologies again.

Step #11: We sought through prayer and meditation to improve our conscious contact with God as we understood Her, praying only for knowledge of Her will for us and the power to carry that out.

This is your spiritual practice, and if you don't have one, the twelve-step program literally gives you one. If you think a twelve-step program isn't for you or you don't feel quite ready to attend one, return to chapter four and review the spirituality and mindfulness approaches that were discussed there. Those could be the spiritual practices you engage in every day to help you through your recovery.

Step #12: Having had a spiritual awakening as the result of these Steps, we tried to carry this message to alcoholics [food addicts] and to practice these principles in all our affairs.

Look for a sponsor who has what you want. It took all my courage to approach someone and ask her to be my sponsor. She was so gracious and said yes! She told me to call her every day at 6 a.m. Six in the morning! I don't need to get up at 6 a.m., I thought to myself. And what are we going to talk about every day? But I was willing. I really wanted to recover. I wanted to be sane with food, and I knew I couldn't do it alone. So I called her every day, no matter what was happening in my life.

Her name is Rose, and after each of our daily check-in calls, she would say to me, "Put this on your cheek, Sandra" and made a kissing sound. It was the first time in my life I had a female figure looking out for me, believing in me, and telling me the hard truths. Why would Rose spend years being my guide? That's the beauty of the twelve-step community; we each have a responsibility to guide people down the path of recovery. We must give away our recovery in order to keep it.

It's Your Time to Decide

Now that you know the twelve steps, I have a question for you: Are you open to attending a twelve-step program?

This is something for you to decide, and you only. I know I've learned enough through twelve-step programs to continue my recovery and help others like you in the process. Twelve-step programs are communities ready to welcome you and provide the support you need.

Right now, we're at a place where you need to take some action, and I think it's important for you to know this:

Knowledge alone isn't enough.
You need knowledge plus action.
This will give you lasting change.

I hope you have maintained an open mind about the third pillar of Food Addiction Recovery. With this knowledge, recognize that, yes, you have an affliction called "food addiction," but the problem does not define you. It is not who you are, and it is okay to step out of your comfort zone and consider a twelve-step program.

Overeaters Anonymous has been essential to my journey towards food serenity and recovery. I went to OA for my eating and quickly realized that I needed the program even more for my thinking. The twelve steps raised me up and gave me a blueprint for how to live my life. My parents were not able to guide me or raise me, but the people in OA did. Along the way, I learned I had a lot more to work through. I realized I was codependent and had trouble setting healthy boundaries. I was raised to be a people pleaser, and that led me into a lot of conflict and pain. My next steps were to learn how to set boundaries, how to love myself, and how to be assertive. I am grateful for this program and the loving people in it who helped me grow into the woman I am today.

Now that we've covered all Three Pillars of Food Addiction Recovery, I'll recap them here:

Three Pillars Of Food Addiction Recovery

RECOVERY
PEACE/NEUTRALITY WITH FOOD

Eliminate Trigger Foods

Develop Spirituality & Mindfulness

Belong To A Support Network

CREATE AN INTERNAL ENVIRONMENT THAT IS KIND, GENTLE, AND NURTURING TO HELP ENSURE SUCCESS

Pillar One: Eliminate Trigger Foods

You are not the addict voice telling you to give into your cravings. You are the voice of reason trying to shut down that addict voice. Don't forget that you are capable of staying calm and confident in the face of a craving.

Pillar Two: Develop Spirituality and Mindfulness

When your mind is full of love and light for yourself and those around you, the addict voice becomes a whisper. Each day, spend time in meditation, connect to the Divine spark you were born with, and find the calm, wise, and peaceful core of yourself. Live from this place, select food from this place, and eat from this core.

Pillar Three: Belong to a Support Network

Having people who are there for you in your recovery is essential. They empower you to keep going and recognize your efforts, no matter how hard things get. They also keep you from falling back into old habits and appreciate the beautiful, resilient person you are becoming.

Before I could begin implementing the pillars in my life, I needed to prioritize myself. I lived for my mother. Her needs took precedence over all else, preventing me from attending to my own wellbeing. In the next chapter, I describe how I immersed myself in recovery, established loving boundaries with my mom, and accepted that I could not save her in order to spare myself the same sad fate.

Chapter Five Exercises

Exercise #1: Believe in Miracles

You are the architect of your life. Every structure begins with a thought. Then the architect takes pen to paper to draw out her idea. No one stands behind the architect and says, "There's no building there—it's just a pile of dirt." Our new life begins with a thought, a thought brought to life on paper, a belief that this new life is possible.

It starts with a thought.
It's designed on paper with great detail.
Then, it comes into manifestation.

I want you, if just for a moment, to believe that a miracle has occurred. The miracle is that your problems with food are gone, and you have healthy, beautiful relationships with your body, with God, and with food.

Define your Higher Power:

_____

_____

_____

_____

_____

What does this Higher Power want for you?

_____

_____

_____

_____

What do you want from this Higher Power?

_____

_____

_____

_____

Describe the relationship you want with food.

_____

_____

_____

_____

Exercise #2: Build Your Village of Support

My village started in the rooms of Overeaters Anonymous, where I took my first baby steps towards food serenity. I stopped weighing myself and instead focused on developing a healthy relationship with food and myself. I learned about the importance of getting proper sleep, developed a sustainable meal plan, and started exercising regularly.

Take a look at the village of support below. I want you to give each element a score out of 10. A score of 0/10 means you are struggling with that aspect of your health, and a score of 10/10 means you have mastered the element.

Your Village of Support

List the areas of your life that received low scores and outline your plan to address them and build your village of support:

_____

_____

_____

_____

_____

_____

_____

_____

_____

_____

Checking in with Jannet...

Remember Jannet from the introduction? I received an email from her recently in which she shared her progress with me. Here is what she wrote:

Today I have completed five full years sugar "sober," and it dawned on me to look back through my journals with the daily recording I learned from your course. It's great to feel healthy, to be entirely free of the joint, back, and other pain I experienced ninety-plus pounds ago. I now have energy and sleep better because I am not burdened by the additional weight I carried for decades.

Last week, I read an article about Body Mass Index (BMI), and I realized that all this time, my focus has been about staying the course I committed to when I left your first class—to abstaining completely from sugar and refined carbohydrates. One meal at a time, one day at a time, one month at a time, I have focused only on the goal of breaking the cycle of addiction that started in infancy as soon as I was placed on baby formula, which was replaced by processed foods in childhood, and then substituted for tobacco and alcohol as an adult. Although I long ago broke free of my addictions to smoking and drinking alcohol, there seemed no way to avoid food.

Since the start of your program, I have weighed myself at the conclusion of each thirty-day cycle, saying a small prayer before stepping on the scale to have courage to accept the number I will see there. I then record this number like a Life Lab book entry to mark progress on my weight-loss journey. I also document how my physical body and emotional spirit are feeling. The number was not intended to indicate where I am in some self-defeating race to the "finish line," but when it didn't change for several months, I struggled not to judge myself or doubt the efficacy of the program.

Well, my body-weight has now remained consistent for several months, and this article about a healthy BMI prompted me to see where I am on the scale. I am in the "normal" range between BMI readings of 18.5-24.9. It then dawned on me to check my monthly weight recording to see how long I have been in the healthy BMI range for my age and height. It has been eighteen months! In other words, during the last third of this five-year journey (to date), I have had a healthy BMI.

It's hard to describe the impact that realization had on me as well as how thankful I am that I learned about you. I was inspired by your personal story, which prompted me to commit to your program and follow its guidelines. It's not a race, but when you have achieved a particular goal—like crossing a finish line in a marathon—then realize you had already won the race two thirds of the way through the course, there is a tremendous sense of confidence that arises within. I demonstrated to myself (even if unconsciously) that this is my actual "normal." I am free of the symptoms and cravings of addiction. I can focus on living a full life with a whole array of new possibilities because I am healthier, stronger, moving better, sleeping better, and living without the pain of both cravings and the physical side-effects of a BMI that places me in the overweight or, in my experience for over a decade, obese weight classification.

Thanks again, Sandra. I hope the courses you teach will help others the way they have helped me and that they continue to reinforce my personal journey towards food sobriety.

CHAPTER SIX

FOOD ADDICTION ROBBED ME OF MY MOM

Tape Reel: In My Mother's Eyes, JULY 1980

I'm standing at the front door of my home, and I don't want to go in, but I'm twelve years old, and I don't have a choice. I slowly reach my hand for the cold bronze knob, and my heart begins to beat faster. I hold my breath for a few moments…not knowing what will be on the other side of the door. Will I find my mother singing happily, her spirit soaring with hyper-confidence? Although the prospect is somewhat pleasant, it is also frightening. "She is in a good mood. You should be happy," I try to convince myself, but her temporary high is only a mask that conceals her deep shame and sadness.

I knew it would not be long before the mask came off. There were times when I found her sobbing inconsolably. In these moments, she had little to no desire to go on. There were times when I entered an environment of pure rage and screaming so loud that the windows rattled. My house was filled with the chaos of ups and downs and everything in between. I pleaded to God, "Can today be the day I find Mom singing Italian songs at the top of her lungs, buzzing around a symphony of delicious smells and a stove full of bubbling pots?" Or my favorite of all, "Can today be the day I come home to the solace of the sound of sizzling, breaded eggplant, softly set in the pan to fry?"

My mother lived with bipolar disorder and morbid obesity, and at the tender young age of four, I remember feeling deep loneliness for the first time, looking for someone to care for me, engage me, and love me. I was the baby of the family, with three much older siblings, and yet, I was the neglected child, the dirty kid at school, with little knowledge or exposure to any other way of life.

One of my earliest memories was looking around the living room and trying to find my place. One of my sisters had been removed from our home by Children's Aid. My other sister sobbed. And my brother, the only person I felt safe with, was nowhere to be found.

My childhood home did not have a foundation, not in the figurative sense. It was not an emotionally safe place. In my mother's eyes, I did not see my worth reflected back at me, and I became a sponge to the trauma of my home life. The pieces of my peace were scattered everywhere, and at a young age, I struggled to find a way to collect them and achieve peace with myself and my environment.

Thinking back to a warm summer afternoon in 1980, I sit with my Raggedy Ann doll on a velour couch watching General Hospital, *a show far too sophisticated for this eight-year-old. My mother calls me into the kitchen, grabs my arms, and presses play on her favorite tape of self-loathing: "Sandra, what have I done with my life? You need to help me," she pleads. "Can't you see I'm sick, and need you to help me?"*

I was desperate for my mom's love, so I reversed roles with her at a young age. I thought if I could care for her perfectly, if I could be perfect enough for her, then she would get better.

And if she got better, she could love me. When that didn't happen, I believed it was my fault. I decided I was not worthy of love, and I carried this belief into adulthood and into many of my relationships.

Often our childhoods determine whether we will develop codependency in adulthood. Think back to your early years. Did you feel safe in your home? Did your caregivers struggle with addiction or mental health? Was there a lot of fighting in your home? Did you think it was your job to make things better? Did the chaos in your home make you feel like you didn't matter? Did you feel like your experiences were not important? Perhaps no one paid much attention to you except, maybe, when you were being helpful? Were you a mature child? Did you have to grow up quickly and take care of your siblings and/or parents? Did you feel like you were never enough? You couldn't do enough or be enough to make things better? Were you allowed to be sad or express your feelings? Did you feel seen, heard, valued?

Webster's Dictionary defines codependency as "a psychological condition or a relationship in which a person manifesting low self-esteem and a strong desire for approval has an unhealthy attachment to another, often controlling or manipulative person (such as a person with an addiction to alcohol or drugs)."

Many food addicts grow up in highly dysfunctional homes. They are never given the security and guidance all children deserve. They take on the pain and weight of the entire family's trauma.

In my case, eating for comfort made those years bearable. My siblings and I were able to survive by reaching for the most accessible substance available to us—food.

That little girl trying to save my mom became an adult woman trying to save my mom, and I almost lost my life trying.

Have you ever tried to save someone, to make someone happy?

What about living for someone else?

In my experience it doesn't work—and it's heartbreaking.

Saving Mom

It's 3 a.m., and my phone rings. It's dad. Mom isn't right. The adrenaline pulls me out of bed and into the car on a cold winter's night. The drive to their house is a short one, and my mind is racing.

This has been the story of my entire life—caring for my mother, who lives with obesity and bipolar disorder.

Tonight she has gone into diabetic shock.

I arrive to find her naked, strewn across the couch in the basement, disoriented and in pain.

My hand shakes as I struggle to dial 9-1-1. We wait, only to have the paramedics arrive and say, "She is too heavy for us to lift. We have to call the fire department."

Shame washes over my mother. Two years later, obesity would take her life at the age of sixty-nine. I could not save her.

People spend a lifetime looking for their purpose. Some climb Mount Kilimanjaro and ask the heavens. Others spend seven years in Tibet. Some *Eat, Pray, Love* across the globe. Not me. At eight years old, my purpose was handed to me on a platter. I put Raggedy Ann down, tightened my pony tail, and went to work.

My life's purpose was clear. I was going to save my mom, and if I could make her better, I would matter.

I breathed in that responsibility. That day, I stopped crying every time I heard my mom cry. That day, I no longer felt frightened when she banged her head against the wall and said she wanted to die. I had made a decision. I was responsible. I had to make her better.

As the years went on, the weight of my responsibilities grew. Six a.m. alarms went off daily so I could get to Mom's before work to administer her meds. I always remembered to check under her tongue to ensure she really had taken them.

Every Friday night, I pulled into her driveway, bags packed in the backseat because I needed to babysit her for the weekend. She didn't want to be alone. Meanwhile, five blocks away, my husband sat in our home alone. I spent weeks at a time at her bedside in psychiatric wards while doctors tried to find that perfect cocktail of mood stabilizers and antidepressants to sustain her.

I was committed to my life's purpose. I was going to save her. And so began a codependent relationship that would take ten years to untangle.

Codependency and Boundaries

Codependency

It is easy to confuse codependency and our values: *I want to help others. I want to be remembered for being kind. I should be a good daughter, son, parent, or sibling.* In codependency, we use those values as our reason to give beyond what is reasonable. We honor our values when we say, "Give me your hand. I will help you." However, when that person begins to take us down with them, it is time to let go.

A therapist recommended I cut my mom out of my life completely. Although things were unbearable and continually in crisis, I knew I couldn't bear the idea of not helping my mom when she was suffering. I had to find a way to honor my value of being a good daughter without allowing my mom's illnesses to swallow my entire life. I could not sacrifice my health and wellbeing by putting my mom's needs, health, and crises ahead of my own. Instead, I made a list of how much I could comfortably give my mom in terms of time, energy, and financial resources. Before making this list, I needed to ensure my tank was full. What did I need to be healthy, happy, and fulfilled? Once I met all my needs, I could gauge what was left to give. That's what I called *my good daughter quota.* It also alleviated my guilt. Once I hit my quota for the week in terms of what I set out to give, even if she called and begged or things got crazy, I said no. Mom had to find another way to get help once I gave what I could.

I realized that every time I rescued her, I robbed my mom of the chance to get better on her own. When we rescue people, we enable them to stay stuck and, thereby, rob them of growth. We prevent them from learning to assemble their own resources for managing their afflictions. Understand that when you decide what your own *quota* will be, you must adhere to it, no matter what.

So many of us have it backwards. Often women fall victim to ensuring everyone else's needs are met, paving the way to make life easier for others, softening life's lessons for those we love. We think that once everyone has what they need and once everyone is taken care of, we will finally look after ourselves. But by the time we get to ourselves, we are exhausted, resentful, and empty.

You can think of a codependent relationship as a partnered dance. One dance partner gives too much, makes herself too available, feels responsible for everything, and the other dance partner takes too much, demonstrates helplessness, uses guilt and manipulation to get their way. When you start setting boundaries on how much you can give your partner, their life will seem to fall apart: The dependent will lose their job, a pipe will break in their home, their dog will need surgery, or another catastrophic event will occur from which the dependent will beg you for rescue. "It's different this time…" you think to yourself. But it never is.

Boundaries

I think people get a little confused about boundaries, and I want to give you my explanation.

Often people believe *others* must adhere to their boundaries. But ultimately, we are powerless over the actions of others. My definition of boundaries is establishing what I am comfortable giving and how I keep myself well and safe. How much money am I comfortable giving, how much time can I spare, and how much energy can I offer? And sometimes I cannot give anything. Boundaries keep me emotionally and physically safe. And once I reach my limit, I have to enforce my own boundaries and stop giving.

I am the keeper of my boundaries, and I need to walk away when they are crossed. I cannot force anyone to honor my boundaries; it is up to me. I want to pause here and note that if someone is breaking the law or harming you, you may need to do more than walk away. You may need to call the authorities.

Let me explore ghosts of Christmases past with you. I would describe Christmas time with my family as a time of dread, fear, and ALWAYS weight-gain for me. It never ceases to amaze me how much weight I could gain in that two-week period. My mother's bipolar disorder cast a dark shadow over the holidays. It is a family disease, and we suffered along with her. Each of her children worked hard to walk a tightrope—one missed step, and my mother would explode. The holidays meant my dad had time off work, so the chances of domestic violence were real. We could not achieve peace in our home.

How did I go from feeling miserable during the holidays to enjoying them more than any other time of the year? In one word: BOUNDARIES. I am Italian, so some aspects of my cultural upbringing did not set me up to enforce healthy boundaries. I remember the first time the concept was introduced to me at a therapist's office.

The therapist asked, "Do you know what a boundary is?"

I (suppressing a laugh) innocently answered, "Do you mean like a border… like the one between Canada and the US?" That was the only boundary my family respected.

Boundaries meant I decided what kinds of behavior I would tolerate. This decision did not change because of circumstances. I would not be disrespected or abused.

PERIOD.

It did not matter if it happened at home, at work, or with friends. I took the same stance. It's a matter of self-preservation.

We often have to create boundaries with emotionally unstable or unwell people, so communicating these boundaries can be difficult. As an adult, I no longer tolerated verbal abuse from my mom. This was not a boundary I could communicate to her; it would have been explosive. She would have been furious at the mere suggestion that I thought she was verbally abusive. I had to set my boundary, and I had to enforce it. Each time my mom would start in on me, I needed to leave the situation. I did my very best to excuse myself in a gentle and kind way. I would not get into the reasons why. I would not give her anything to fight against or argue about.

This. Was. Not. Easy.

When the verbal abuse would start, I would leave her home, and she would have an adult tantrum. Many times, I thought it would have been easier to just ignore it or put up with it. But I could no longer prioritize her feelings above my own because each time I did that, I needed to compulsively overeat to numb the pain. I had to walk through the fire to be free.

The last time my mom was verbally abusive toward me, as I slowly reached for my purse, she said, "Don't go. I'll stop." It was a freakin' miracle.

What Happens When Someone Does NOT Respect My Boundaries?

My life experience has shown me that I often have to create boundaries with those who are emotionally unwell. Because I am the creator and enforcer of my boundaries, I must have a plan of action for times when someone crosses them. This is not to fight or tell them off. I simply remove myself from the situation or relationship because I determine it is no longer safe to share their company.

The road to a healthy relationship with my mom required boundaries. Boundaries make us, and those around us, feel safe. They allow us to build trust with ourselves, and as a result, others trust us when we say something because they know we mean it.

The time came when I decided it was best for my health and wellbeing that I no longer slept at my mom's on weekends. Friday night rolled around, and my phone rang.

"Sandra, I can't move my left arm," Mom cried into the phone.

Due to diabetes, my mom suffered many mild strokes. Now I am faced with the decision to either enforce my boundary or get in my car and drive the mere five minutes to her house to "save the day."

I check my watch: 7:05 p.m. I take a breath and reply, "Ma, we have two options. We can go to the walk-in clinic or to the emergency room. Which one would you like?"

I hear her let out a long sigh, followed by, "I want you to sleep over."

So here it was.

"I can't do that," I reply calmly.

Cue her reaction: "I am going to die! This time is different! What kind of daughter are you?"

It didn't matter I had already given fifteen years of my life to waiting on her hand and foot. I had spent countless weekends at her house, and every Sunday as I was getting ready to leave, I had to hear her plead, "Please don't go. If you go, I am going to die. Please don't go."

It wasn't enough. It would never be enough, and for many reasons, she would not see my side of things. Her reaction would be adverse so long as I adhered to my boundary.

She finally slammed the phone down. Conversation over.

We both lay in our beds that night crying. It was hard for me to draw this line with her. But I did. What if she died that night? It would have been my fault—or so I thought. I had to learn I was not that powerful. I could not save my mom or cause her death. I surrendered to that fact. I fully placed my mom in the hands of God to keep her safe. It was no longer my job. I was not sleeping over this time, and I would never again stay over for the weekend.

Time passed. During my first year of recovery, I spent only Saturdays from 12 p.m. to 4 p.m. visiting Mom in her home because I could not stop using food if I was my mother's full-time caregiver.

Once when I was getting ready to leave at the regularly scheduled time, I approached the top of the stairs and saw my mom standing at the bottom, looking up at me. "Oh no, what is it going to be this time," I thought.

"Sandra," she said softly. "I want to thank you for spending the afternoon with me."

My knees nearly bucked. I had spent years battling her through the "don't go's" and now, after some time of giving first to myself and what I had remaining to her, she thanked me.

"You're welcome." I smiled.

This was the first time in my life she had ever thanked me for anything.

This boundary allowed my mom to trust me. In time, she was able to trust that my no meant no and my yes was genuine. There was safety in that no for her, finally.

Is Everything My Fault?

I have a childhood friend I love dearly named Luana. Luana transferred to St. Raphael Catholic School in grade seven. Up to this point, I really didn't have any friends. In the early years at school, I struggled with neglect, which meant I was the dirty kid who wore the same clothes to school each day. This coupled with an undiagnosed learning disability made matters even harder for me. I have dyslexia and struggled with reading and writing.

I was instantly drawn to Luana. I knew in my heart she would be my BFF.

We instantly became like sisters.

What I didn't know at the time was that we were actually experiencing similar childhood traumas. We were both living in violent homes with an emotionally unavailable parent. Her dad and my mom shared so many similarities, and we were both children trying to save our families. So looking back, I see how easy it was to become fast and wonderful friends.

Luana's father was mentally ill and emotionally unsafe—like my mom—so Luana made herself responsible for *everything*, and this responsibility is something she still lives with. Whenever Luana made dinner plans for us, she held herself responsible for any imperfections that occurred throughout the evening. If the service was bad or the food wasn't great, her night would be ruined, and she would suffer from the guilt of a "failed" outing. Luana absorbed blame for things completely unrelated to her and fully beyond her control.

So I want you to ask yourself this: Do you see a little bit of Luana in yourself? Do you feel at fault for things completely out of your control? Do you feel anxiety, pity, or guilt when other people have a problem? Are you compelled to help them solve it?

Do You Struggle to Trust Your Gut?

Whenever I'm having a conversation, and I get this uneasy feeling inside that I can't identify, I recognize that something isn't sitting right with me. I know that I should not decide on the topic at hand right away. Often I ask the other person if I can have one or two days to think about the conversation, digest the information, and return to them with my decision.

This strategy is also a wonderful test to determine who you're working with and what kind of relationship you share. If the person says, "No, you can't have more time. I need an answer now," this is a big red flag. More likely than not, this relationship is unhealthy. If the person says, "Of course, take all the time you need," then it is a good sign because your request has been respected.

Oftentimes if you're experiencing an uneasy feeling, it's because your body's signaling to you that something is not right. Asking for time allows me to discuss this feeling with a mentor or counselor. More often than not, they point out that the situation I was in probably involved some kind of manipulation. It's thanks to that wiggly feeling that I've been able to take a step back from potentially harmful situations or conversations, and I think this is important to mention.

It's so crucial to listen to your body. It shares tons of wisdom though sensations, even if you can't articulate what you're feeling. Often to survive our tumultuous childhoods, we had to disconnect from our bodies, our instincts, and our inner voice. Now that we are adults, we can start to reconnect to our inner wisdom. It does take practice and sometimes guidance from a counselor. But doing so will help you avoid unhealthy relationships and ensure your boundaries remain intact.

Do You Value Others' Approval Over Your Own?

Valuing others' approval of your thinking, feelings, and behaviors over your own is what I like to call "putting your self-worth on a platter and shopping it around." If you find yourself in a room with ten different people, are you concerned with what each person thinks of you? Do you want each person in the room to approve of you, like you, and make you feel okay about yourself? If there's even one person with a negative opinion of you, will you hyper-focus on them and figure out why they don't think you're okay? Will you think this person has ruined your day? Will you continue seeking their approval, as well as the approval of others, until you feel like you've either gained it or your self-esteem has crumbled even further?

People pleasers are often codependent, meaning they seek validation from others. This need for approval can lead them to put the needs of others above their own. They might go out of their way to help people, even if it means sacrificing their own time and energy. Codependent people often have trouble saying no, even when they really want to. They might stay in unhealthy relationships or tolerate bad behavior because they fear being alone. While codependent people pleasers might feel they need others to be happy, this is not true. They can find validation and approval from within themselves. By setting boundaries and giving themselves permission to say no, codependent people can start to live healthier, happier lives.

Navigating Relationships

As a small child, I tried to make sense of my sad world. I rationalized that if I could be perfect, then I could be loved, and I carried that belief into adulthood. This set me up for a lifetime of rejecting love from others and myself. I recreated scenarios that mirrored my codependency with Mom in every relationship I had. I chose men who could not love me, who were emotionally unavailable, and I kept trying to be perfect enough to change them. I saw things as I wanted to see them instead of the way they actually were. Part of my recovery was detaching with love.

Detaching with love comes from a place of deep acceptance, acceptance of a person's decisions, actions, and lifestyle. Everyone is free to choose how they wish to live, and we must respect that freedom. This is a tall order, especially when we can clearly see that someone we care for is making decisions that cause them pain, and we think we can make it better. Ultimately, each of us has a unique path we're meant to follow, and our journeys will all look different. We cannot force anyone onto the path we feel is best for them.

Sometimes we will witness our loved ones make mistakes, fall down, and suffer. Can we be okay with that? Every time we "rescue" someone, we rob them of a learning experience and growth. We enable them to stay stuck. Can you courageously apply the principle of "Live and Let Live," even when it's heartbreaking?

Thankfully, I made my peace with my mom before she passed away. I remember looking at her. Diabetes had ravaged her body. She could not walk unassisted, her eyesight was minimal, she was incontinent, and her shirt was always dirty. She had lost all her teeth and food would run down her top. I looked at her in her totality, and I accepted her exactly as she was. I loved her exactly as she was. I surrendered to her life choices and where they had brought her. I released my mom, and I released myself. I tell you the story of my mother, not to disparage, but to honor her. She was my greatest teacher, and I will forever love her. She is gone, and I believe she is whole again, and we can know each other in a new way.

True love is unconditional, something I have longed for since childhood. And I was slowly dying from the lack of it.

My way out was to love myself. This way, I didn't need anyone to give love to me, and no one could take it away from me. It would become the new way I related to myself.

Through the eyes of acceptance and kindness, I saw the best in me, and that brought out the best in me. I reclaimed my human-ness, which means I accept that I will never be perfect. I will never look perfect, act perfectly, or eat perfectly. And this imperfection makes me lovable. A newfound freedom was born!

Tape Reel: Epiphany at 40,000 Feet, FEBRUARY 2001

I board a plane to Arizona. I'm twenty-nine years old and 100 pounds overweight. I am miserable. I am depressed. My marriage is crumbling, and the damn seatbelt will not fit. I refuse to ask for a seatbelt extender, so I hide the seatbelt under my belly flap. The flight attendant doesn't notice, and shame washes over me.

Shortly after takeoff, the plane hits turbulence, the kind that ensues terror. The attendants scramble to their seats, and all I can do is grip the armrests.

I hang on and hang on, and it is exhausting. My life is exhausting. I can't do it anymore. At forty thousand feet in the air, I can finally see clearly. My mother was self-destructing. She was going down, and I was going down with her. She gave that eight-year-old an impossible task. I couldn't save her and had spent years believing it was my fault.

The plane touches down safely, and by the time it does, everything for me has shifted. I begin my journey back to myself, the road paved with self-love and self-acceptance.

I stop using food as a drug, end my family legacy of addiction, and reclaim my purpose.

The Greatest Gift

Food addiction took my mother's life. Because of her food addiction, her life was not truly lived. And neither was mine. I will never know the solace of a mother's hug, know the safety of confiding my deepest fears to her, or know the rejoice of celebrating success with my mom. On the day my mother passed, I began my journey to bring meaning to her life. I wasn't able to save Mom, but in many ways, I'm still trying to through the clients I serve.

My mother's death certificate will never say food addiction was the cause of death, but I know, and now you know, that it was what killed her. The greatest gift my mom could have given me was to have lived a healthy, fulfilled life, where her happiness was a priority. This would have changed the trajectory of both our lives.

We are all searching for unconditional love. My journey has taught me that until I am able to give it to myself, I cannot give it to another or receive it. It all begins with me.

The greatest gift I can give—to myself or to anyone else—is to step into my power, claim my gifts, and live my own life's purpose. These are now the gifts I give my daughter.

I think back to another warm summer afternoon. This time, I watch as *my* eight-year-old runs ahead of me along the Toronto Beaches' boardwalk, giggling as her kite dances in the blue sky. I call her over, and she runs toward me. I wrap her in my arms. "I love you," I whisper. "I want you to have your own life," I say as she smiles, wriggles free from my arms, and returns to admiring the swooping movement of the wings and tail of her kite. I breathe in serenity. Sofia is free.

As a child, coming home after school was a scary thing for me. Today, when I hear my daughter place her key in the door of our home after school, I make my way toward it and make sure to greet her with love. My daughter doesn't wonder what she'll find on the other side of the door. My eyes reflect her worth. She hears it in my voice but also sees it in my actions. She is brilliant, full of personality, the single greatest blessing of my life, and I love every piece of her. I do all I can so that she believes **she is enough**.

In the next chapter, we will delve deeper into the effects codependency has not only on your relationship with food but also on your relationships with others. I will share how my codependent relationship with Mom impacted my romantic life in particular and provide you with tips for developing healthier bonds with both food and people.

Chapter Six Exercises

Exercise #1: Strike a Balance Between Your Values and Self-Love

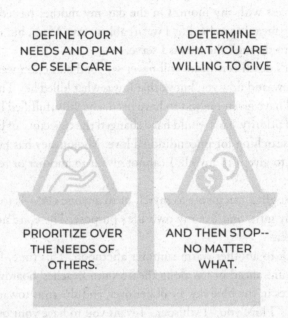

DEFINE YOUR
NEEDS AND PLAN
OF SELF CARE

DETERMINE
WHAT YOU ARE
WILLING TO GIVE

PRIORITIZE OVER
THE NEEDS OF
OTHERS.

AND THEN STOP--
NO MATTER
WHAT.

The purpose of this exercise is to determine how to balance your self-love and self-care with helping others. When doing this exercise, I want you to consider someone in your life with whom you struggle to maintain boundaries, someone who often leaves you depleted.

First thing's first—define what your needs are. Start with the basics: sleep, healthy meals, time spent outdoors, meditation, and movement.

Step #1: List your needs to be well:

_____

_____

_____

In a codependent relationship, both individuals tend to overlook their own needs in order to please the other person. As a result, each person ends up feeling drained and resentful. If you find yourself in a codependent relationship, it is important to take a step back and assess your needs. What are you sacrificing in order to keep the other person happy? Is it your time, your interests, or your dreams? Once you have identified your needs, you can start taking the steps necessary to fulfill them. This may mean setting aside time for yourself, pursuing your own interests, or communicating your needs. It is also important to remember that you cannot make the other person happy; only they can do that. By taking care of yourself and setting boundaries, you can begin to build a healthier, more balanced relationship.

Step #2: What am I willing to give?

Identify a person or institution (i.e. work, church, etc.) with which you may be codependent.

Now consider how much time and energy you have left to give after all your needs are met. What can you comfortably give in terms of time, energy, and sometimes even finances? You may also find that it's better not to give in this situation, and that's okay.

Time

_____

_____

_____

_____

_____

Energy

_____

_____

_____

_____

Finances

_____

_____

_____

_____

This is your quota for helping this person or institution. Once you've reached your quota for the week, month, or year (whatever you set out), then it is time to release this person or institution to find their own way. Otherwise, you may be robbing them of the opportunity to grow stronger. This is not an easy road, but it is often the road to freedom for you both.

Meet Andy

If I had to describe what life and my relationship with food were like before working with Sandra, I would say that it was a lonely and difficult experience. I struggled with food addiction and compulsive eating and as a result, weighed 300 pounds. Obesity, diabetes, and weight were always issues in my family, so I felt like I was destined to follow in those footsteps. However, with Sandra's help, I realized there was another way. Through kindness, love, and wisdom, Sandra showed me how to recover from my food addiction and start living a healthier life. Now I am finally free from the chains of compulsive eating and am learning to love myself and my body.

When I was deep in the throws of food addiction, I felt incredibly alone. I didn't know there were other men like me who were battling the same issue. I felt like a failure because no matter how successful I was, people only saw me as obese. I couldn't see myself past my flaws and thought recovery was impossible. The reality is that food addiction is a powerful force, and it takes more than willpower to overcome it. I am so grateful to have found recovery, but it has been a long and difficult road. There are still times when I falter, but I am no longer alone on my journey.

When I started my business, I was ashamed of my food addiction, my compulsive eating, and my body. COVID gave me an excuse to hide—it was the perfect storm. I could expand my business from behind my computer without having to put myself out there. I even hired someone else to be the face of my business.

I was never taught that food addiction is a real disease. I thought I was just weak and lazy. Despite trying every diet, reading every success book, hiring every coach, and attending every conference, no one ever told me there was science behind my behavior. Even my doctor didn't know about it. If they had, maybe I could have been helped sooner. Maybe I could have avoided years of suffering.

For most of my life, food was simultaneously my enemy and my crutch. I was addicted to the highs and lows of compulsive eating, and my relationship with food was one of turmoil and pain. I thought that if I stuffed myself with food, I wouldn't have to feel my feelings. Binging numbed me, disconnecting me from myself and others. Rather than admit I had a problem with food, I blamed everyone else for my problems and felt like a victim. I was in a dark place and didn't see any way out.

But then I met Sandra and began to develop a new relationship with food—one that was based on nourishment and self-care. Slowly but surely, I began to heal. Sandra helped me see that food addiction is a real thing, and that it's not my fault. She gave me tools, like breathing techniques and self-affirmations, that have really helped me in my recovery. Sandra also encouraged me to throw out my scale and stop counting calories. Instead, she taught me to focus on making healthy choices and listening to my body.

I have lost seventy pounds and have finally found peace with food. I don't beat myself up anymore. Instead, I focus on the present moment. This presence helps me stay mindful of what I'm eating and also helps with my anxiety. Now I savor my food and use all five senses when I eat. When I take the time to slow down and really taste my food, it is so much more satisfying. I have also learned to trust myself around food. I used to think that certain foods were "off-limits" because of all the diets I had tried. When I was consumed by my eating disorder, I was obsessed with food, and restriction felt like a way to control my life. But now I know that food is just food. It's not good or bad. It's fuel for my body.

CHAPTER SEVEN

FOOD, LOVE, & RELATIONSHIPS

66 Your task is not to seek for love,
but merely to seek and find all
the barriers within yourself that
you have built against it."

– RUMI

Tape Reel: Going to the Chapel, OCTOBER 1992

I'm twenty years old, standing at the chapel doors in a big white wedding dress with a four-foot train. There's a man at the end of the aisle whom I do NOT want to marry. How did I get here?

First, I need to tell you where I'm from. I'm from a mom whose mental illness made her emotionally unavailable to me. My needs to be seen, to be heard, to be loved were too much for her. So she put her needs on me. She wanted me to take care of her and to make her happy. We reversed roles, which I welcomed, as it eased the pain of being neglected. I truly believed if I could be perfect enough, take care of her perfectly, she would get better and give me the love I desperately wanted from her. This didn't happen, and I thought it was my fault. I wasn't enough.

I'm from a father who didn't sign up for this kind of marriage. He was rageful and violent and stole my sense of safety at the age of four. I've since learned children need to feel special, safe, and loved. This way, when they become adults, they will reject any situations that do not make them feel special, safe, and loved.

The opposite was true for me. I continuously put myself in situations where my partner did not make me feel special, safe, or loved. It strangely felt like home. So when I was sixteen, and someone looked into my eyes and said, "I love you" for the first time in my life—well, you know I was going to marry him.

Going back to my wedding day on that sunny October afternoon, I remember the moment before the chapel doors flung open, my beautiful, hopeful twenty-year-old face fell in total despair. My father stood next to me as I tried my best to divert my eyes away from the videographer who was beginning to lose hope that I would gaze with excitement into the camera. My face remained sullen and unchanged as we awaited the sound of the organ, signaling it was time to go inside.

My only relief came from knowing I could always get divorced, which allowed me to pull up my expression for just a few brief moments.

As you probably guessed, I did walk through those chapel doors that day. My four-foot train heavy with the weight of one thousand hesitations and my despondency dragged down the aisle to meet and marry a man who was so much like my father. We divorced by the time I was thirty years old. Seven years later, I was engaged to a man who was just like my mother. That relationship ended by the time I was forty years old, at which point, over two decades of my life had passed where I sought out the only kind of connection I knew—the kind that had been modeled by my parents. I had erected so many barriers to love, and it was clear my work here had only just begun.

What are your barriers to love? Do they sound something like this?

I am not thin enough.
I am not lovable enough.
I am not smart enough.
I am not pretty enough.
I am not rich enough.
I am not young enough.

These are all lies we tell ourselves. Are you ready and willing to let go of these lies? Because when you let go of them, what is left is you. Being vulnerable is often one of the hardest things to do. Who are you when you drop the lies? Let's find out.

- Close your eyes and take three deep, grounding breaths.
- Next, turn your attention to your heart. Place your left hand over your heart.
- Envision your heart opening.
- For it to open, try thinking of what you need to let go of.
- Do you feel safe enough to open your heart? What do you need to undo? What are your barriers? What have you told yourself about being worthy?

You must untangle yourself from all of the *never enoughs* and detach yourself from how you think about love. I won't mislead you—undoing these beliefs can be painful. But once you do, you will find your true self. The "you" who has been there all along, waiting for the moment you decide *you are deserving of love.*

Can you trust your heart to remain open? Can you trust that you won't put yourself in situations that dishonor your magnificence? Real love is not rescuing others, nor is it accepting bad behavior. We can love, and we can be safe. For many years, I believed my heart was too broken to be open and vulnerable. I felt I couldn't trust it to make good decisions. The connection between my heart and my head was broken. I sometimes couldn't see the truth of a relationship because I was desperate not to be alone.

Today, I know my heart is whole, and I'll be bold enough to say your heart is whole too. We've disallowed the connection between our heart and head and failed to trust our inner knowing. But that can stop today. We were born with an enormous capacity to love. Our hearts are powerful.

Beliefs are thoughts based on past experiences that you repeat over and over until they become hardwired into your brain. Can you rewrite your story about love? What beliefs do you hold?

- If I'm critical with myself, I will be critical of another.
- If I'm impatient with myself, I will be impatient with another.
- If I'm unhappy with myself, I will be unhappy with another.
- If I'm happy with myself, I can be happy with another.
- If I love myself, I can love another.
- If I'm at peace with myself, I can be at peace with those around me.

The Lies We Tell Ourselves

Often to ease the pain of living a dysfunctional life, we lie to ourselves. If you are in a bad marriage, you might be lying to yourself about just how helpless it is by choosing to ignore the facts that are right in front you.

If you work in a toxic environment, you may think there is no other option. It will be nearly impossible to avoid comfort eating if an area of your life is unbearably painful. So I really want you to examine where you might be lying to yourself and convincing yourself to stay in these unfulfilling and destructive situations.

A Life in Review

I have an assignment for you. I want you to shine a light over your entire life and look for areas that are dysfunctional, where you might feel broken and in pain. Why? Because addiction is about pain relief, and when you are in pain, you are in jeopardy of using food to alleviate and numb this pain.

I have five questions for you to answer that may uncover areas of your life that are dysfunctional or toxic.

Everyone has areas of their lives that they are working on, and this is normal. Recognize that these questions point to ideal situations, places we strive to be in our lives:

- Are you in a relationship that nurtures your spirit and enhances your life?

- Does your career inspire you?
- Do you have the necessary boundaries in place to live a healthy, whole life?
- Do you care for and nourish your body, mind, and spirit?
- Are the thoughts that occupy your mind energizing?

To survive a dysfunctional lifestyle, we must lie to ourselves. What lies are you telling yourself about the broken areas of your life in order to make them bearable?

Want to Know Why You Abuse Food? Stop Abusing It.

If you want to know what drives you to abuse food, the quickest way to find out is to stop abusing food. When you stop abusing food, the reason(s) you have "used" it in the past come bubbling to the surface.

This was certainly the case for me. Once I stopped eating compulsively, I realized that I was experiencing paralyzing fear. It was a fear that I hadn't felt in over twenty years. To feel an emotion that has been dead for so long, buried by food for so long, was crippling for me. Fear was my biggest driver to use food for comfort.

Numbing Your Feelings with Food

The day you start using food to cope with your life is the day you begin stunting your emotional maturity. I started using food to cope with everyday life when I was about twelve years old. If I got a bad grade at school, I had no one in my life I could turn to for help. I would go home and compulsively overeat until the bad grade didn't matter anymore.

As I got older, I carried this coping mechanism with me. When I was dating and my boyfriend and I would have a fight, I would go home and eat a whole pint of ice cream until it didn't matter anymore. I didn't learn to apologize or to communicate effectively. Instead, I ate until I had numbed out my feelings. When I got my first job, whenever I made a mistake at work and felt embarrassed, I would go home and compulsively overeat.

By the time I was thirty and had finally stopped abusing food, my toolbox for life was empty. I didn't know how to communicate effectively or face all the uncomfortable things I was experiencing. I had missed opportunities to learn how to own my mistakes and clean them up. As life presented opportunities for me to grow and mature, I used only one tool, one solution to fix everything: food.

You have the power to decide what you think, and the way you think will often determine the way you feel. Choose your thoughts wisely. "If everyone would just behave and not piss me off, and if work weren't stressful and my family didn't dump on me, I could be skinny!" said foolish twenty-something Sandra. This used to be my favorite excuse. I would say, "Don't you know I have a terrible husband and my mother guilts me daily and work is overwhelming? I have to eat." I would say, "It's all your fault that I'm eating this way, that I'm carrying all this extra weight." I was marrying my emotions to my eating habits, and it was destroying my life. If my food serenity depends on everyone behaving in my life and life being a smooth ride, I'm in real trouble.

I had to learn to untangle the mess I had made. My emotions, the ups and downs of life, had to be kept separate from my eating plan. This required some high-quality thinking. Chances are, if you feel you're having a crappy day, your thoughts are crappy too. But it's important to understand that you have the power to decide what you think, and the way you think will influence how you feel, and then your actions are often affected.

This isn't about just engaging in positive thinking—it's about seeing all sides and asking what else could be true in a situation. It's about remembering the power you hold to change the way you think about something in order to reorganize your emotions depending on the situation.

Here's another example: I have chubby thighs, and sometimes they rub in hot weather. Jeans don't always fit right either. The truth is, yes, I have chubby thighs, and sometimes they cause me discomfort, but what else is true? I can choose to focus on the fact that I have super strong legs.

I can wear four-inch heels for an entire day. I ran a half-marathon. I can do squats, jumps, lunges, and dance. The takeaway here is this: While everything I've just stated in regards to my thighs and legs is true, it is the kind of thinking I engage in that decides the way I feel about my thighs. When I decide to entertain negative thoughts about my thighs, I show up in the world differently. But seeing everything that's right and beautiful about myself makes me walk differently, makes me show up in the world differently, and engaging in this thinking attracts beautiful things to me.

The Great Offenders: Fear, Anger, and Resentment

Fear, anger, and resentment are absolutely normal human emotions, and I think this is something essential to mention before I dive into this topic. I'm not here to tell you not to experience these emotions. That would be absolutely ridiculous because we're all human. But what I am here to tell you is that if you identify as a food addict, these emotions are more difficult to manage. What I want to offer you are new, fresh perspectives on these emotions.

> 66 Whenever you feel angry or fearful, whenever you feel guilty or disappointed, you're—in that very moment—achieving harmony with what you don't want."
>
> – ESTHER HICKS Sara,
> Book 1: The Foreverness of
> Friends of a Feather

Fear, anger, and resentment have a lot to do with your perspective of yourself, your personal world, and your beliefs about your fellow human beings.

Fear and Faith

Consider that fear is often focused on the future, what could potentially happen, what could go wrong, what could be missed or messed up. Resentment is often focused on the past, the wrongs done to us, things taken away from us. Both fear and resentment have little to do with the present moment.

So let's begin by looking at fear. Fear is often about a future situation you think you won't be able to handle. It's difficult to predict what will be available to you in the future; it's hard to figure out where your strength, inspiration, and resources will come from. In this present moment, you can allow the Divine to show you the way, give you the strength, and provide you with the inspiration to carry on. The Divine is always in the present moment.

How is your fear tied to your view of the world and your place in it? Do you believe that your personal world is kind, loving, and supportive? Do you believe that you will have everything you need for each step you take? Have you ever taken a step in complete faith, not knowing what would happen but trusting that everything would work out? The act of taking that step can be frightening, can't it? But sometimes we need to take a leap of faith.

Thankfully, this universe is kind, loving, and supportive. It will provide us with everything we need for each step we take. Allow the right people to come into your life, the right way to reveal itself to you, and the right doors to open for you. Can you trust that everything will work out exactly as it should? So the next time you're feeling scared or unsure, remember that this universe has your back. Trust that all you need is already within you. Just take that first step in faith, and watch the healing unfold.

Can we experience fear and faith at the same time? At this very moment, as you read these words, all is well. When we stay present, we may find that the things we were afraid of were not as frightening as they seemed. Instead, they were simply False Evidence Appearing Real.

American religious leader Russell M. Nelson famously said, "Faith is the antidote for fear."

Faith is an interesting thing.

By definition, it is the belief in something without proof. It is trusting that even when we can't see the whole picture, things will work out in the end. In many ways, faith is the opposite of fear. Fear focuses on what could go wrong while faith inspires us to believe that everything will be alright. Faith is a decision to have hope, even when everything around us tells us to give up. It's saying, "I'm going to choose to believe that this situation will work out, even though I don't know how."

And oftentimes, that decision is enough to change the outcome.

When we choose faith over fear, we open ourselves up to possibilities instead of limitations. We become willing to take risks and follow our dreams. It's not always easy, but it is always worth it.

So the next time you're feeling afraid, remember Nelson's words: "Faith is the antidote for fear." Choose faith over fear—always—and watch your life change for the better.

Letting Go to Receive Love

Let's look at resentment and anger and how they are tied to our beliefs. There's one camp that believes there are some rotten apples when it comes to people. And there's another camp that believes we are all born good—and then stuff happens to us.

No one goes to the maternity ward and says, "Look at these sweet babies" while thinking to themselves, *this one is an angel, but that other baby is evil.* We all come into this world perfect beings, understanding our worth, filled with promise for a bright future.

So why would people hurt each other? Let's be clear: Those who hurt others are, themselves, in great pain. Often they are sick. It's not a sickness we can see, but if you believe we all come into the world "good," then we need to believe that if a person is causing us harm, something has gone wrong. And it is likely something completely outside of this person's control. At this point, we must accept that the harm we are experiencing is unintentional. We are collateral damage. We must also face the fact that we, ourselves, hurt people unintentionally, likely due to our unhealed wounds.

Anger and resentment are barriers to love, and love is essential for recovery. When we are angry and resentful, we are focused on ourselves and our own pain. This focus prevents us from seeing the love that is all around us. It also prevents us from giving and receiving love. Instead of being open to the love of others, we close ourselves off, furthering our isolation. In order to recover from food addiction, we must be open to love. We need to let go of anger and resentment so that we can see the love that is already present in our lives.

The Big Book of Alcoholics Anonymous says resentment is the number one offender. Why? It can eat away at us, causing us to feel angry and alone. It can distort our perception of reality, causing us to see the worst in people and situations. And it can lead us to say and do things that we later regret. In short, resentment is a poison that can destroy our lives. But there is hope. The good news is that we can choose to let go of our resentment. We can choose to forgive those who have wronged us, even if they never apologize, because we understand they are too sick to say sorry. We can choose to move on with our lives. Sometimes it comes down to this decision: Do you want to be right, or do you want peace?

> **❝** It is plain that a life which includes deep resentment only leads to futility and unhappiness. To the precise extent that we permit this, do we squander the hours that might have been worthwhile.
> But with the alcoholic [food addict], whose hope is the maintenance and growth of a spiritual experience, this business of resentment is infinitely grave."

– THE BIG BOOK OF ALCOHOLICS ANONYMOUS

Untangling the emotions that lead you to compulsively overeat and learning to manage them will take you far in both your life and your recovery journey. Food serenity is more than just finding peace with food—it's also about finding peace with yourself and others. I know this is something you can do. It's the reason you've picked up this book, and I'm here to tell you that you can achieve it.

The Practice of Letting Go

One of the most difficult things in life can be learning to accept people and situations that we don't necessarily agree with or like. But as the old saying goes, "Acceptance is the key to happiness." And while it's often easier said than done, there are ways we can learn to accept things beyond our control. For me, one of the most helpful things has been reading *The Big Book of Alcoholics Anonymous*. In it, there is a small passage about acceptance that really resonates with me. And if you're struggling to accept someone or something in your life, it may help you shift your perspective on the situation and let go of the negative emotions that are weighing you down. Here's the passage:

And acceptance is the answer to all my problems today. When I am disturbed, it is because I find some person [insert person's name], place, thing or situation—some fact of my life—unacceptable to me. I can find no serenity until I accept that person [insert person's name], place, thing or situation as being exactly the way it is supposed to be at this moment. Nothing, absolutely nothing, happens in God's world by mistake. Until I could accept my [food addiction], I could not stay sober; unless I accept life completely on life's terms, I cannot be happy. I need to concentrate not so much on what needs to be changed in the world as on what needs to be changed in me and my attitudes.

If you're struggling with one person in particular, I suggest you insert that person's name into the passage as shown above. I experienced great healing from this exercise. Inserting the person's name into this passage helped me understand that they're exactly where they need to be and freed me to focus on myself and my attitudes. I was able to shift my perspective and manage my thinking so I wasn't living from a place of fear, anger, and resentment. Instead, I was compassionate and living from a place of peace.

Remember, faith over fear. So often in life, we are faced with choices that seem impossible. It can be incredibly difficult to muster up the courage to take the first step, but it is always worth it in the end. When we have faith, we are able to see past our fears and doubts. We are able to see the potential for what could be. Having faith doesn't mean that we will always get what we want or that things will always go our way, but it does mean we can trust that everything happens for a reason. Even when things are tough, we know that there is light at the end of the tunnel. We know that better days lie ahead. As we look back on hard times, this perspective will enable us to find meaning in the pain we once perceived as senseless suffering.

Anger and resentment often result from fear. Your anger is likely proportional to the fear you're experiencing. When we feel threatened, our natural reaction is to lash out in order to protect ourselves. However, this can often do more harm than good. Not only does it damage relationships, but it also makes us feel even more afraid and alone. The next time you find yourself feeling angry or resentful, ask yourself what it is you are really afraid of. Once you identify the root of your fear, you can start to work on addressing it. This can be a difficult and scary process, but it is crucial to your recovery.

Commit to the next right decision, just for today. It's easy to get caught up in what we perceive as the "right decision." We agonize over every little choice, big or small. But the truth is, there is no such thing as a universally right decision. There is only what is right for you at this moment. And when you commit to making the next right decision—just for today—the universe will support you every step of the way.

The path may not always be clear, but if you trust your intuition and stay open to guidance, you will always find your way. Take a deep breath and let go of your need to control the outcome. The only thing you can control is your next right decision.

I believe that challenges do not keep us from our dreams but prepare us to meet them. This belief was put to the test when I struggled with food addiction. For years, food was my enemy. I would yo-yo diet, restricting food intake only to compulsively overeat and feel out of control again. I was consumed by food and my weight. I felt like a failure.

But somehow, I held onto the belief that this challenge was not going to keep me from my dreams. It was preparing me for something bigger. And eventually, with the help of many and a lot of hard work, I was able to develop a healthy relationship with food.

Today, I am living my dreams and helping others do the same.

I am no longer fighting food or fearing food; rather, I've made peace with food. And I am grateful for that challenge because it prepared me for this moment in my life.

So, When Do I Meet Mr. Right?

I'm ready to meet "Mr. Right," so I asked myself, "How do I attract my soulmate?" Well, that's a big question, and I always take big questions into meditation. This was where I heard the answer: *Lean back and receive.* At which point, I asked myself, "What does that even mean?" Lean back and receive? Aren't I supposed to work for it? Aren't I supposed to be perfect? Was I not supposed to prove my worthiness of love? Then I realized that finding love and loving myself means letting go of everything I knew about love.

But can everything I believed really just be washed away? Can the doubt of my worthiness be washed away? Can the fear of truly being seen, heard, and loved be washed away? All of it, washed away…until I am left with just me? In that stillness, that quiet, I heard the truth. *I am a beautiful being deserving of love.* And so are you. For no other reason than because *you* are *you.*

Finding love is not easy when we carry the weight of our childhood traumas and the anger, fear, and resentment that accompany them. I have made peace with my childhood, myself, and my need for love. Therefore, the next time I get married (and there will be a next time), my vows will sound like this:

> *Dear One,*
>
> *I love you so much that I am going to put myself first.*
>
> *I promise to be at peace with who I am so that I can be at peace with who you are.*
>
> *I am committed to my greatness so that I can be comfortable with your greatness.*
>
> *I take full responsibility for how I feel about you. It's all on me.*
>
> *The only thing I ask of you is that you do the same for me.*
>
> *Now I am open, willing, and ready for love.*
>
> *With love,*
>
> *Sandra*

Imagine yourself now, leaning back and receiving love.

Even when you open yourself to this unconditional love for yourself and others, you may falter on your journey towards food serenity. In the next chapter, I will discuss my experience with relapse and equip you with some strategies for returning to the path of recovery should you relapse.

Chapter Seven Exercises

Exercise #1: A Life in Review

- Are you in a relationship that nurtures your spirit and enhances your life?
- Does your career inspire you?
- Do you have the necessary boundaries in place to live a healthy, whole life?
- Do you care for and nourish your body, mind, and spirit?

- Are the thoughts that occupy your mind energizing?

To survive a dysfunctional lifestyle, we must lie to ourselves to make the chaos bearable. What lies are you telling yourself about the broken areas of your life?

_____

_____

_____

_____

Exercise #2: Proud of Myself

This next exercise is very powerful if you suffer with low self-worth. Each night before you fall asleep, I want you to review your day and pick one action that you are proud of. Next, and this is the most important piece, identify what this action means about you and who you are becoming.

For example, if you completed the exercises in this chapter, you can record that accomplishment as something you are proud of. When answering what this means about you, you can list qualities like those found below:

- Committed to getting better
- A hard worker
- Open
- Seeing possibilities

I AM PROUD OF MYSELF TODAY FOR:

....

....

....

....

....

THIS MEANS I AM:

☑ SMART ☑ CAPABLE

☑ CARING ☑ STRONG

☑ FUNNY ☑ CREATIVE

☑ LOVING ☑ BRAVE

...AND SO MUCH MORE!

Meet Mike

After decades of searching, I finally found the right support to get me off the never-ending diet rollercoaster and adopt lifestyle changes that have enabled me to achieve lasting recovery from food addiction. I am now free from what I initially thought was weak willpower but later learned was an addiction to certain foods and behaviors over which I was powerless. Since I learned that I was a food addict and found the right combination of professional food addiction treatment and extensive work in a focused, twelve-step recovery group, I have made some dramatic changes to the way I eat and how I manage my emotions surrounding food.

While people who struggle with food addiction come in many different shapes and sizes, both before and after finding recovery, my greatest concern was always my weight. I felt that if I could just fix my weight, life would be so much better. I would be so much happier and so much more deserving of love. I spent most of my adult life at or above 300 pounds at 5'10," with my maximum weight pushing somewhere close to 400 pounds, although I stopped weighing myself after I reached 360 pounds.

Despite wanting to lose the weight, I felt that nothing I tried ever worked or stuck. I might have lost the occasional twenty to thirty pounds but almost always quickly gained it back, or more, in a very short time.

I was a chubby kid and teenager who felt horribly insecure, primarily because of my weight.

From as early as I can remember, I was obsessed with food. Both of my parents were addicts, and I believe I inherited my addictive tendencies from them. I always wanted to eat as much as I could, particularly if it was something I enjoyed. My family raced through dinner to secure the largest possible portion of second helpings. They frequently had cookies, donuts, and other junk foods in the house, and I constantly got into trouble for either eating more than my share or eating everything. Though my parents consistently punished me for my gluttony, I remained undeterred. Even when my parents locked food in their bedroom, I managed to eat it. As early as age ten, I stole money from my mother's purse to buy more sweets. The tremendous joy and comfort I received from food overshadowed any guilt my actions incurred. I was an active and athletic child, but by the age of eleven, I really started to notice myself growing chubby and began my first actual diet. That first diet didn't work, and neither did any other I tried until age forty-five, when I finally found food serenity.

Even worse than the physical and mental struggle of the weight was the way I felt about myself.

I often beat myself up for what I considered personal weakness. Everyone but me seemed to maintain healthy relationships with food and lose weight relatively easily. Comparing myself to others made me feel very depressed, which frequently led me to seek comfort from food, perpetuating a vicious cycle of binging followed by fruitless dieting.

I even admitted himself to eating-disorder treatment centers on several occasions. Despite learning a lot from these experiences, their impact never endured once I returned home. I attended hundreds of eating-disorder recovery meetings, hired a nutritionist, and worked diligently with my sponsors to no avail. My chronic relapses led me to treat myself with cruelty. I felt like a truly helpless case.

On May 7th, 2018, everything changed for me in a dramatic and unbelievable way. I attended a twelve-step food recovery meeting and saw a glow of recovery and confidence in the speaker that I wanted for myself.

The speaker approached me after the meeting and gave me two assignments. The first was to read the Doctor's Opinion in the *Big Book of Alcoholics Anonymous* and see whether I could relate the high alcoholics get from drinking to the high I get from eating. The second was to identify my trigger foods.

I followed the speaker's advice and embarked on my journey to cut out all trigger foods from my diet. The first few weeks were painful and uncomfortable, but I approached my recovery one day at a time. Very quickly, I began feeling better than I ever had before. I started attending daily twelve-step meetings and adopted a wholesome eating plan designed for my ideal weight. I stopped weighing myself and started working vigorously on a spiritual program guided by my sponsor and support team. My program is called SMERF, which stands for Spirituality, Meditation, Exercise, Rest, and Food Plan. Adhering to it has grown progressively easier for me over time and has ultimately become a beloved way of life.

Today, after several years of complete abstinence from my trigger foods, I have lost 150 pounds naturally and feel healthier and happier than ever. Despite facing many obstacles on my road to recovery, I am now a certified food addiction counselor and yoga instructor.

Most importantly, I have learned to love myself. I encourage anyone who struggles with food addiction to persevere through their recovery so they can achieve the same peace with food, others, and themselves that I have.

CHAPTER EIGHT

THE ROAD TO RECOVERY IS OFTEN PAVED WITH RELAPSE

"It is always darkest before the dawn."

– THOMAS FULLER

Relapse is part of almost every addict's journey, including the food addict's. The way we treat ourselves *during* a setback will determine how quickly we get back on course. Relapse is often framed as a failure, and it's a bit of a taboo topic. Many believe that if we don't talk about relapse, it won't happen." But that's kind of like thinking if we don't talk about sex with our kids, it won't happen. We all know how that turns out.

According to *Merriam-Webster*, relapse is defined as "the act or an instance of backsliding, worsening, or subsiding and a recurrence of symptoms of a disease after a period of improvement."

It is not defined as a failure, as something shameful, or as a disgrace. That's how we addicts define it, and seeing relapse from this perspective will keep you stuck and in pain. It's hard to get better when motivated by shame, guilt, or hate.

I don't wish a relapse on anyone. But I want you to know it is a normal part of the journey should it happen to you. I want you to see relapse or a setback as an opportunity for growth.

Each of my relapses was a signal to go deeper in my healing. It's also an opportunity to forgive ourselves and move forward with our healing. So if you find yourself struggling, remember that you are not alone and that relapse is not the end of the road.

The words we speak to ourselves are powerful, so I am careful as I choose them. I wish to speak words that are kind, necessary, and truthful. I choose to frame a relapse this way: "It was a moment in time, and it's gone forever. It's also a chance for rubber to hit the road of unconditional love and acceptance. It's easy to love ourselves when all is well, but true love means loving ourselves when we fall down."

I encourage you to choose your words carefully as well.

Years ago, I hosted a radio show called "Your Daily Diet: A Spiritual Guide to a Healthy Body Size." My vision was to create a community that, together, would reclaim our power over the diet industry and media's beauty standards. The community would define beauty and set the standard for self-love. To find peace with food, peace with ourselves, and ultimately, peace with those around us.

Each month I would feature an interview with an expert who introduced new ways of relating to food and our bodies. I loved this experience because it was more than just a show.

"Your Daily Diet" was fundamental in bringing together a community of seekers open to finding a solution beyond dieting, aimed at healing the Mind, Body, and Spirit. This community is truly my people!

One day I received a touching email from a listener. It read:

> Dear Sandra,
>
> I have fallen into the dark hole. I have lost control of my eating AGAIN. I don't know how to stop. I don't know why I started, and it is killing me—robbing me of days, robbing me of time with my kids, robbing me of my self-respect. I have relapsed back into compulsive overeating. I am filled with shame. I feel worthless. If I don't use food, I sit on the couch overcome by depression. If I give in, I lose another precious day of my life, a day gone forever. I cannot afford to lose any more days. I will never know how much my addiction has cost me, and I continue to pay the price.
>
> My mind keeps playing tricks on me. It tells me I can handle pastries, French fries, and ice cream. My mind tells me that I need to learn how to enjoy them in moderation, and I should be a normal eater. But one taste turns into an uncontrollable drive to eat as much as possible until I am too sick to continue. I feel like an animal. I eat everything I can get my hands on, whether I am hungry or not. I resolve never to use food again, and my mind taunts me and says, "YES, YOU WILL." I feel I have to be locked away to stop.

I replied to this email, knowing that I have been exactly where the sender is, and offered the following advice:

> Dear Jamie,
>
> Thank you for this honest and vulnerable email. You are not an animal, but your animal brain has taken a hold over you. Let me explain. Food like pastries, French fries, and ice cream are chemically engineered foods never found in nature with too much fat and too much sugar for our brains to handle. When our ancestors came across naturally occurring foods high in calories and sugar, their animal brains (or more accurately, their mid-brains) would go into overdrive and allow them to eat as much as humanly possible. Their brains would override the full feeling because they needed to ingest as many calories as they

could. It was a matter of life or death. This drive still lives in us today. The problem is, there's a fast-food joint at every corner and a bakery on every block.

Every relapse starts with a lie—a voice in your head that says, "This time, it will be different. You can have just a little, and you will be fine. Look at everyone around who can enjoy delicious food and be just fine." This experience is no different than a person living with alcoholism watching someone enjoy one glass of wine and feeling desperate to be able to do the same. But it will never be this way for them. How do you live with this voice and make peace with it?

Here's what I have discovered: Anything I fight against fights back. Anything I resist persists. I understand that my mid-brain's job is to keep me alive, and because of this drive, I can no longer expose my brain to chemically engineered foods (i.e. junk food). I have lovingly decided that it is easier and kinder to eliminate exposure to these drug foods the same way a loving parent shields her child from street drugs. When I am enticed to take a bite, I speak gently and lovingly to myself. I give my midbrain the reassurance it needs—I am safe, and I will survive. I recognize this faulty thinking and know it could cause compulsive overeating. I practice not reacting to this voice and allow the urges to fall away. I pour as much love as possible into this part of my brain, which has gone awry.

To quote one of my favorite spiritual teachers, Deepak Chopra, "The solution never lies at the level of the problem; the solution is always love." I spend time in meditation each day to ask Divine powers to heal the part of my brain that drives me to use food.

My hope is that you understand the role chemically engineered food plays in compulsive overeating, find a community to walk alongside you, and learn how you can heal with love.

I experienced my first relapse after eight years of recovery, eight years of abstinence from compulsive overeating, eight years of working my program and going to meetings, eight years of food freedom. This relapse lasted a year and half, far longer than it should have. The shame, embarrassment, and isolation of it kept me stuck in relapse and tremendous pain. After eight years, how could I go from winning at overcoming my addiction to falling back to where I started, eating compulsively for comfort?

I just want to pause here and let you know it is a fallacy to believe we go right back to where we started. This is a low-quality perspective. You never go back to square one. You can never unlearn the things you've learned. You can never undo the steps forward you've taken. Relapse doesn't mean senseless suffering. You can find meaning in it.

This major relapse happened after the end of a significant relationship. After the breakup, I wanted to take a considerable amount of "me" time, time for self-care, for adventure, and for pushing myself out of my comfort zone. I did some traveling on my own. I attended a ten-day silent meditation retreat. I had always wanted to run a half-marathon, and now I had the time to train for it. Completing the half-marathon was solely about accomplishing a really big self-care goal. Training for it resulted in a lot of weight-loss, but this was not my motivation to run. As you know by now, my weight is none of my business. My business is to eat whole foods and move my body regularly, and wherever my weight ends up, my job is to love and appreciate the body I have.

I ran the half-marathon in September. As the weather progressively became cooler, I needed warmer clothes. One morning, I went to put on a pair of pants, and they nearly fell off me. For the first time in eight years, I really, really, really wanted to know what I weighed. I figured it had to be good news.

I lied to myself. I told myself I would be fine, that this time would be different. I could handle it. This is the same lie I told myself for years about my trigger foods, and that day I used this lie to engage in trigger behavior once more. I stepped on the scale, and I weighed 130 pounds. I hadn't weighed 130 pounds since grade seven.

So what do you think my reaction was? Most of you might expect that I would be ecstatic and excited, that I would be beaming because I was at my lowest adult weight ever. Instead, I was disappointed.

My goal weight for many years when I was compulsively dieting was 120 pounds, and now I was only ten pounds away. I was so close—maybe I could finally get to that magic number, the goal weight that was going to give me everything I ever wanted in life. This number held such meaning for me because I believed that when I reached this weight, I would find the love of my life.

I would have an exciting career. I would be seen, heard, and loved.

The number on the scale never made me happy. It never mattered what number showed up. It was never going to be enough. After stepping off the scale, I made a decision that was the absolute wrong thing for me to do. I would focus all my attention and energy on losing the last ten pounds. There's a saying in the twelve-step rooms of Overeaters Anonymous: "When we focus on losing weight, we lose recovery." This decision to chase down the last ten pounds would cost me dearly.

At this time, I was a member of Overeaters Anonymous. (I am not a member of any twelve-step program today.) At this point, I noticed that people were leaving OA to join a new twelve-step program with prescriptive meal plans that produce significant weight-loss. It is important to note that I'm going to tell you about my specific experience with this fellowship in 2010.

I went to my first meeting at this new fellowship shortly after deciding I needed to lose ten pounds. I arrived at my first meeting and looked around. It seemed everyone was very thin at this meeting. I wanted that. The first order of business was to get a new sponsor—no waiting on this one. My sponsor was going to give me a meal plan, which was pretty much the same meal plan everyone in the room followed. This should have been my first clue that things weren't right. It is absurd to believe that every food addict can follow a similar meal plan, considering people's ages, health concerns, cultural backgrounds, etc. My sponsor not only gave me a meal plan, but she told me what I needed to weigh to be considered in recovery. For my height, I was to weigh 112 pounds. WOW! This was even better than my goal weight. Sign me up!

Starting the next day, I followed a very strict, regimented diet. I was told to let go of exercise because it would make me hungry. At the time, I didn't realize what a devastating blow that would be. Up until this point, I was very active, having just completed the half-marathon. As winter was approaching, I had taken up weight lifting. But most importantly, exercise was my natural antidepressant. This essential tool for regulating my mood was being taken away from me by my new sponsor.

This meal plan was not enough food for me. The red flags were apparent: I was constantly hungry, I had trouble falling asleep at night because my stomach was growling, I stopped menstruating, and my hair was beginning to thin. All this did not matter to me—all that mattered was getting to my goal of 120 pounds.

Eventually, I did get to 120 pounds, but that wasn't enough. My next goal was 112 pounds. Yet again, the number never made me happy. I was playing with fire, adhering to a restricted diet is a dangerous game to play. When we restrict our calories too much, our brains believe we are experiencing a famine. This was a self-imposed famine, but my brain had no idea. The only reason you and I are here today is because our ancestors were able to survive famines.

This restrictive diet caused a cascade of events in my brain that drove up my hunger, pushing me to seek food and eat as much as possible. Because our brains are efficient, I desired calorie-dense, sugary foods. My brain believed it was a matter of life or death.

Every Relapse Starts with a Lie

I woke up on a Saturday morning in the Spring of 2010. I ate my breakfast at 6:30, and by 10:30, I was hungry again. I felt like I was starving. My brain started cycling through different lies. I started to think I could have some more breakfast. I could have some fruit. But I was committed to the eating plan given to me by my sponsor. I didn't want to break my abstinence; I didn't want to "give away" my recovery. I was brainwashed into believing that eating off the plan, even whole foods, was a relapse, and relapse would be my fault. Had my plan been reasonable, had the plan been created by a medical professional, an apple would have been totally fine, and adding more food to my plan would have made sense.

Then, jackpot—or so I thought. My mind came up with a lie that I fell for. I convinced myself that just for this weekend, I would eat whatever I wanted, that it would be different this time. Anyways, how much weight could I gain in two days? At this point, I was still just concerned about my weight and thought it had nothing to do with my relationship with food. Plus, I had the magic meal plan that was going to get me to 112 pounds that I could start again on Monday morning.

All my old thinking patterns had returned in full force.

I believed the lie that it would be for just two days, and it was like the pistol at the start line—I was off to hunt down my "drug foods" like a junkie looking for her next fix. I ingested foods that I hadn't had in eight years. I got incredibly sick but could not stop. There were moments when my heart was racing. I felt like I would pass out from all the sugar I was dumping into my system. I began throwing up, not because I wanted to, but because I just couldn't keep the food down. Then I was out the door to get more "drug foods." And more. And more. The food was so UNsatisfying. I was chasing euphoria, but I couldn't find it in the food.

So the lie that it would last for only two days—well, that relapse lasted for a year and half, and I gained seventy pounds. The most difficult part of the relapse was the shame and embarrassment I carried, which stopped me from seeking help. I thought I had to stop on my own. I thought that when things got back on track, I would return to meetings and ask for help. I felt I couldn't let anyone see me like this.

I didn't reach out for help until, once again in my life, I arrived at a place where I honestly didn't care if I ever lost another pound again. I just couldn't keep eating the way I was eating, and I couldn't keep living the way I was living. I had to build a village of support around me again. I had to forgive myself and practice unconditional acceptance and love for myself again. Why? Because love is energizing. I needed all the energy I could muster to get back on the road to recovery.

This painful relapse wasn't senseless suffering. I found meaning in it. As a result of this relapse, I came to terms with the fact that twelve-step programs were no longer for me and don't work for everyone. I gave birth to my Food Addiction Recovery Program, and that later inspired me to write this book.

I know you're intelligent. You already likely know what to eat and what not to eat, and you know exercise is a good idea. My program is about the "how" of living healthfully—how do I stick to my plan when I'm overwhelmed, scared, lonely, or when life gets in the way? (To learn more about my programs, visit sandraelia. com.)

One of the most difficult things about recovery is that it rarely follows a straight line. There are ups and downs, relapses and setbacks. But even though relapse can be discouraging, it also serves an important purpose. It can be a wake-up call, telling you that you need to go deeper on your journey of healing.

Relapse can be an opportunity to learn more about yourself and what triggers your addictive behaviors. With this knowledge, you can begin to build a stronger foundation for recovery. So if you find yourself struggling after a relapse, remember that it is not a failure. It is simply part of the process. Be gentle with yourself and keep moving forward.

Whenever I focused on my weight, I would lose my recovery. And whenever I focused on my recovery, I would lose weight. This is why relapse prevention should focus on your recovery.

Make it your number-one priority. Don't lose sight of self-care and growth. You've come a long way, and I know you have the tools and self-love to keep going.

Revisiting the Pillars of Recovery

We are going to return to the Pillars of Recovery to help set ourselves up for success, and I invite you to create your own plan for recovery along the way.

Pillar #1: Eliminate Trigger Foods

Trigger foods are foods that you obsess about. Once you start eating a trigger food, it is difficult to stop. Eating your trigger foods often leads you to compulsively overeat other foods. These foods almost always contain refined sugar and refined flour.

Looking at the first pillar, eliminating trigger foods, it's important to have a plan for what you eat. You can keep it simple and eliminate refined sugar and flour and eat whole foods, you can follow a meal plan from a twelve-step program, or you can talk to a healthcare provider and design a plan that will work for your body and your lifestyle. It's important to understand your specific needs and to build your plan to eliminate trigger foods around them.

Everyone needs a plan of eating. I'm so fortunate to be a great-aunt. It warms my heart to watch my nieces prepare meal plans for their toddlers, meal plans with the right combination of protein, vegetables, fruit, good carbs, and fats.

Why?

This way, the children will flourish and be healthy. The need for a meal plan doesn't disappear when we grow older. We need a meal plan through the years that will bring us vitality, energy, and health.

So I want you to figure out exactly how you're going to eat, one meal at a time, one day at a time. Just focus on eliminating the foods that are unpeaceful. At each meal, ask yourself whether you are willing to eliminate trigger foods—just for this meal.

Then ask yourself the same question at the next meal.

One day, you'll look over your shoulder and realize that for days, weeks, months, and perhaps even years, you have been free of your trigger foods.

Pillar #2: Develop Spirituality and Mindfulness

Addictive eating is mindless eating, and one of the antidotes is mindfulness. If you've struggled with your eating or weight for years, maybe even decades, this can clip away at your self-esteem and self-worth.

Spirituality is a healing balm; it is remembering who you truly are. You were born with the spark of the Divine, and that spark still lives in you. Spirituality is about connecting to your magnificence, to a place inside of you that is calm and knowing. A spiritual practice will facilitate a connection to your inner wisdom.

Consider the following when developing your spirituality practice:

- What does your spiritual practice entail (i.e. prayer, meditation, nature, movement, breathing)?
- What time of day will it happen?
- How much time will you give to it?
- What are the steps you'll take to grow your spirituality?
- Will you seek out a teacher or specific practice?

Pillar #3: Belong to a Support Network

When it comes to your support network, it is important to identify a few things:

- Who is in your support network?
- Where do they meet?
- Do you want a mentor?
- Do you want a sponsor?
- Do you want psychological support?
- What does your support network look like?

Once you've answered these questions, it is time to connect with your support network. And if you want, you can always join my support network, which meets virtually once a week, and get all the help and support you need. (Go to sandraelia.com for more information.) By joining my community, you'll have a support network that celebrates your successes and walks with you through your challenges.

There are many contributing factors to food addiction, and it is a complex disease. There's no single answer to recovery. And if relapse enters the equation, it is particularly important to surround yourself with help. Whether through my program or your own mentor, sponsor, or professional help, you set yourself up for success when you let yourself be helped.

We're all trying to reach the land of peace and neutrality with food, and it's through the Three Pillars of Food Addiction Recovery and by using what we've learned—the tools in our toolbox—that we can better ourselves and become the people we want to be. These three pillars are our foundation for building a life of safety and neutrality with food. With this foundation in place, food can assume its rightful purpose, and we can achieve food serenity, where we eat foods that energize, nourish, and vitalize our bodies. We will no longer use foods to alter our state or to escape our pain.

Blessing or Curse?

Now I have a bit of an odd question for you: Is your food addiction a blessing or a curse?

I know what you're probably thinking: *Of course it's a curse. It's ruined my life.* I thought that too. But wait a moment. Don't answer so fast. Instead, actually think about it.

In my twenties, I thought food addiction was the worst curse of my life. And to be honest, if I could've been skinny while compulsively overeating, I would've stayed that way my whole life. I believed that if I could just be skinny, everything else would be okay. But if it hadn't been for my food addiction, I would be nowhere near the woman I am today. I would have never worked on myself. I wouldn't be doing all the things I do to maintain my recovery.

Because of my food addiction, I lead a deeply spiritual life. I practice meditation, eat whole foods, forgive my slips, give myself unconditional love, move my body, and try to be of service. And while I know all that may sound overwhelming to you, it all draws this immense joy to my life that I didn't ever think was possible—a joy I couldn't experience even at my goal weight of 120 pounds.

My food addiction has been one of the greatest blessings of my life because now I'm always searching for meaning. I don't believe in senseless suffering anymore. I broke the cycle of violence, chaos, and addiction, and I'm going to do better for me and my daughter.

I want you to find your why.

My *why* is my beautiful daughter, Sofia, and even though it feels like she does not listen to a single word I say at times, she is studying me and watching me all the time. I know if I want her to grow up and live life loving her body, feeling fulfilled, and prioritizing self-love and self-care, then I must teach her how through my own actions. I must live these things for her to follow them.

My parents never sat me down and said, "This is the way you should treat a significant other. This is the way you need to manage your money. This is the way you handle your health." We never had those conversations, but I watched and learned from them, and what they taught me took ten years of therapy to undo.

I never want to do that to my daughter. I want to show her how to live life by example because she's taking it all in. I never want her to experience the childhood I did, to need years of therapy to undo the chaos I instilled in her life because I didn't know how to love myself unconditionally and live a life of peace.

My food addiction was a blessing in disguise because it taught me everything my parents didn't. It taught me to love myself unconditionally and take care of my body, mind, and spirit. My food addiction and the journey of recovery I've taken have prepared me for my *why*, my daughter, and have pushed me to lead her to live a better life.

Be gentle with yourself; be patient, and most importantly, be proud of yourself for taking this essential first step. By opening this book, you have already shown immense strength and bravery. Nurture your recovery with care and love, and watch it blossom into something beautiful.

In the final chapter, I will share how to build an unshakeable, loving relationship with yourself, one that will endure through any challenges you may face on the road to recovery from your food addiction.

Chapter Eight Exercises

Exercise #1: Uncovering Your Truths

I've shared with you my *why*, my growth, and my tribulations. Now it's your turn to uncover your truths. What is your *why*? What is your inspiration? What's going to keep you going?

Three Pillars Of Food Addiction Recovery

Pillar #1: Eliminate Trigger Foods

- What is your defined meal plan?
- What are your red light foods and green light foods?
- Will you weigh and measure yourself?

Pillar #2: Develop Spirituality and Mindfulness

- What is your spiritual practice?
- What does it entail?
- How much time will you give to this each day?
- What time of day will this happen?

Pillar #3: Belong to a Support Network

- What is your support group?
- When do they meet?
- Where do they meet?

- Do you want a sponsor/mentor?
- Do you need professional help?

Based on the three pillars, create your plan of recovery.

Step #1: Identify and cut out your trigger foods:

_____

_____

_____

_____

Step #2: Design a spirituality practice (where, when, and how will you be mindful?):

_____

_____

_____

_____

Step #3: Develop a support system of people who understand your recovery and will encourage you on the path to food serenity:

_____

_____

_____

_____

CHAPTER NINE

BEGIN A WILD AND UNCONDITIONAL LOVE AFFAIR WITH YOURSELF

Tape Reel: A Revelation in a Church Basement, FEBRUARY 2003

"Love heals all things." These were the words I heard from a gorgeous man at a twelve-step meeting, which was something I attended often for Food Addiction Recovery in my thirties. I can't really remember the content of his speech because I was intoxicated with his looks and charisma. While these meetings were typically attended by women, in comes this beautiful, eloquent man who was going to be our speaker. He too was a recovering food addict, and at that moment, I decided this man was the man of my dreams—the man I was going to marry. All you single ladies out there can relate to getting totally lost in daydreaming about a fictional future, envisioning picnics in the park and long sunset beach walks. My plan was to approach him when he was done speaking and get my flirt on.

As his speech came to an end, he handed out little red hearts he had made by hand using red pipe-cleaners. I remember holding mine and appreciating the time he took to leave us with a little present. At this point he told the audience that he had AIDS and that the significance of the heart was to remind us that Love Heals All Things. Here's a man suffering from an incurable disease with many physical and emotional challenges at the prime of his life, telling me that love heals all things. He will never fully understand the gift he gave me that day. If this was true for him, then this was true for my food addiction.

Now believing this so wholeheartedly, I tell you the same thing: The path to recovery is paved with unconditional self-love, a love that is unwavering. This means you love yourself today the exact same way you'll love yourself when you lose the weight.

Cultivating Unconditional Love

Let's begin the journey to an unconditional love affair with you! This is a love affair where all is forgiven and there are no regrets and no such thing as failure—only lessons to learn a deep acceptance that you are where you need to be. Embrace and cherish all of you, even the lumps, bumps, and stretch marks you may have.

The most important relationship you'll ever have in this lifetime is with you, not your parents, siblings, or romantic partners, but with you! How you relate to yourself will be reflected in your health, your relationships, your finances, and your home. This relationship with yourself is typically given very little attention, time, or nourishment.

Your outer world is a reflection of your inner world. Make no mistake—the way I judged myself in my twenties, weighing more than 260 pounds, was the way I judged others. The self-hatred, the self-condemnation, the harsh internal dialogue I had for myself was mirrored back to me, and I found it everywhere I went. My poor self-image wreaked havoc in my relationships, career, and health. I hated myself. As a result, my body and mind were slowly turning on me and dying.

I had to make peace with myself exactly as I was. I had to love myself at my highest weight the same way I loved myself when I lost 100 pounds and continue to love myself when my weight fluctuates. That is the meaning of unconditional love. The more at peace I am with myself, the more at peace I am with my fellow human beings. When I can recognize the greatness in myself, I'm comfortable recognizing the greatest in others. When I've forgiven and accepted all of my shortcomings, I'm able to forgive and accept your shortcomings.

How does one cultivate an unconditional love affair? Like any other important relationship in your life, it takes time, energy, and patience. What would happen if Ms. or Mr. Wonderful walked into your life? How does one fall in love? You likely already know this formula well. You spend quality time together, you'll see the very best in this person (which brings out the very best in this person). You'll discover what brings them joy and give it to them. Can you do this for yourself?

You are a perfect expression of your Creator, and You are the Creator of your life experience.

With this knowledge comes enormous responsibility, freedom, and joy! It takes courage to stand in the light of day, looking at yourself through the eyes of love to actively seek everything that is right, beautiful, and worthy about you.

Imagine the success you could achieve with your career, relationships, and health if you truly understood your worth and magnificence without condition. The amount of unconditional love and care that is required to set a child up for success is EXACTLY WHAT YOU NEED.

How to Fall in Love with Yourself

Start a love affair with yourself that is unconditional, which means there are no boundaries to your love, because to love yourself unconditionally is to love yourself at all times. Now I don't know about you, but the word "unconditional" makes me zoom in on the parts of me that I put the most conditions on, and this is what I want you to focus on too. I want you to focus on the parts of yourself that cause you the most distress, that are the most embarrassing or shameful to you. These are the parts of ourselves that we just want to hide away forever, but these are the parts of ourselves that are starved for love.

Your body is a living, breathing organism. So if you show hatred to any living, breathing organism, what do you think happens? Well, it absorbs what you say. It's hard to care for something you despise.

We live in a society that is quick to point out our flaws and slow to offer compliments. As a result, it can be all too easy to develop negative feelings about our bodies. However, it is important to remember that our bodies are incredibly efficient machines that deserve our admiration and respect.

The next time you find yourself in front of a mirror, take a moment to really look at yourself—please focus on the parts that have caused you distress. The real work here is to find the beauty and pour love on those areas of your body. Try to see the beauty in all of your features, from your freckles to your curves. Remember, there is no such thing as a "perfect" body—every single one is unique and special in its own way. So love yourself unconditionally, and watch as your world lights up with positivity.

> **"Change the way you look at things, and the things you look at change."**
>
> **– WAYNE DYER**

The first step in this love affair is to forgive yourself. What haven't you forgiven yourself for? What haunts you? Can you forgive yourself for "using" food? Can you see that you were seeking solace in food? Can you have compassion for your childhood, your genetics, and the trauma that may have set you up to develop an addiction to ultra-processed foods? Can you see you've been trying on your own for years, maybe decades, to control this addiction? Can you feel the sadness of knowing there was little help for you until now? Forgiveness leads to total acceptance of where you are now. It is difficult to change what you cannot accept.

Next, let's examine your core beliefs about yourself. We all come into this world as perfect beings, open and receptive to the people and environment that surround us. What happens when your childhood isn't safe, you don't feel special, and love is not showered upon you? Young children need to make sense of the world around them, and as young children, we lack perspective and wisdom. When our worthiness isn't reflected back to us in the eyes of our parents or caregivers, we believe we're not lovable, we're not deserving, and we're not enough. This is especially true if you grew up in a significantly dysfunctional family. My mom's mental illness left her hand print on each of her children. I was certain that the violence was my fault. After every irruptive fight between my parents, I would review my day. Where did I go wrong? What didn't I do? How could I make it stop? If I could just be perfect enough, it would stop, and they would love me.

The beliefs I formed about myself in childhood, I carried into adulthood. I buried them deep into my subconscious mind, and I sought out situations and people that confirmed my beliefs. Doing so felt like home. Unsafe situations, emotionally unavailable men, places where there was little love felt like home. We are all searching for unconditional love, yet we cannot receive it or give it away until we cultivate it for ourselves.

Take some time now to discover your core beliefs. What did you decide as a child to make sense of your world? Have you carried those beliefs into adulthood? Do you choose situations and people to reaffirm those beliefs? Hint: Most humans are plagued with the belief that we are not enough or that we are unlovable.

Now let's focus on your needs. It's time to fill up your tank first before you start giving to anyone else. Are you more concerned with others and their needs? Do you anticipate everyone's needs and fulfill them before anyone even asks? Do you believe you can focus on yourself only once everyone else is okay? If you think this way, know that by the time you get to take care of yourself, you will be completely exhausted and have nothing left to give. You will get up the next morning and do it all over again from an empty tank.

We've all heard the plane analogy: During an emergency, if the oxygen masks are released, you should secure your own first before helping others. Why? Because you can't help anyone when you're unconscious.

Unconditional love is setting yourself up for success. What do you need to be successful? What are the building blocks to a healthy, fulfilling life? Below is a checklist I give my clients, as self-care is often a new idea for so many. The purpose of the checklist is to celebrate your successes each day, big and small. In fact, all major accomplishments are an accumulation of small successes, and we need to recognize them and celebrate each one.

This will help retrain our brains to care for ourselves and keep us moving forward.

ACTION	MON	TUE	WED	THR	FRI	SAT	SUN
GOT TO BED BETWEEN 9 PM - 11 PM.							
WOKE UP BETWEEN 6 AM - 8:30 AM							
MEDITATED (MINIMUM FIVE MINS).							
MOVED MY BODY (MINIMUM TEN MINS).							
SPENT INTENTIONAL TIME OUTDOORS (MINIMUM TEN MINS).							
ONE SUCCESS TODAY.							
ONE THING YOU ARE GRATEFUL FOR.							
PRACTICED SELF-LOVE TODAY.							
MAINTAINED HEALTHY BOUNDARIES (WORK, FRIENDS, PARTNER & FAMILY).							

BEGIN A WILD AND UNCONDITIONAL LOVE AFFAIR WITH YOURSELF

ACTION	MON	TUE	WED	THR	FRI	SAT	SUN
ENJOYED A HEALTHY RELATIONSHIP WITH FOOD TODAY.							
ATE THREE TO FIVE SERVINGS OF VEGETABLES.							
DRANK PLENTY OF WATER.							
CONSUMED ENOUGH PROTEIN.							
ATE MINDFULLY.							
BRUSHED TEETH AFTER DINNER.							

This checklist also serves as a reminder of the steps we need to take to maintain our health, happiness, and success. Never use this checklist to shame yourself or feel bad about what didn't go well. THIS WILL NOT WORK. Look for unhelpful patterns—like if you don't drink enough water, eat in front of the TV, or fail to enforce healthy boundaries on a particular day—does food get really loud for you on these days? This is a data collection tool and will help you uncover high-risk situations and create your unique, tailored plan for recovery.

Let me explain "peaceful relationship with food" and how it relates to this checklist. This doesn't mean a perfect relationship with food! This means, if you have a slip with food, you see it as a moment in time gone forever. You forgive yourself, are kind and gentle (as you're likely suffering). You become present in the moment and move forward. The next moment is a rebirth to live in peace with food.

What's wonderful about this checklist is that it is for everyone. It doesn't matter if you identify as a food addict or not. These are the building blocks to a healthy life.

Set aside time each day to "be" with yourself. This is the quality time needed to begin an unconditional love affair with you. Before you begin each day, spend some time, even moments, to set your intention. Think about who you will see; how you want to show up; and how you can claim Divine intelligence, Divine words, and Divinely inspired actions for the day. Affirm your genuine desire to service the greater good. This time could be your meditation time.

Follow Your Intuition

We are all born with an inner wisdom. I call it intuition.

Intuition is far wiser than education and the Great Equalizer. Intuition is available and accessible to everyone, regardless of age, education, background, or economic standing. I've noticed that most of us don't listen to our intuition and just go through the motions instead of being spiritually connected. We go through life on autopilot.

However, when you meditate and become more present, you allow yourself to see things differently. I want you to connect with your intuition, the inner wisdom inside of you. Start living from this place, and select the food you eat from a place of love and care for your body. When you are quiet and still, you can tap into your intuition. The quieter you are, the louder your intuition becomes. The more you follow your intuition's guidance, the stronger it becomes.

66 The only real valuable thing is intuition."

– ALBERT EINSTEIN

This quote by Albert Einstein has always made me pause to reflect. Albert Einstein was revered for being a genius. I would imagine that he would have been quoted as saying, "The only real valuable thing is understanding the laws of physics" or "possessing a high degree of intelligence." But Mr. Einstein believed intuition is the only valuable thing.

Becoming spiritually aligned with myself and meditating has not only helped me to grow stronger in my Food Addiction Recovery journey, but it has helped me to fully fall in love with myself unconditionally. It has helped me achieve food serenity and approach others from a mindset filled with love and understanding.

Are you okay with yourself in this present moment, as you are in your totality?

I challenge you to put on a pair of glasses, ones that show you that the imperfections, the mistakes, the so-called ugly bits are valuable and are part of what makes you lovable. Put on a new pair of glasses that allow you to see yourself with complete gratitude for who you are today. Look for the purpose these imperfections serve. What lessons can they offer you? How can you be an example for others?

Non-Negotiables

Eating is not a moral issue. Your weight is not a reflection of your worth. Your worth is non-negotiable.

When you eat compulsively...

You're still deserving of unconditional love.

When you binge eat...

You're still deserving of good things.

When you experience a slip...

You're still deserving of compassion.

Chapter Nine Exercises

Exercise #1: Forgiveness

It is time to forgive yourself and to do so in a letter to yourself.

THIS SHOULD BE A LOVING AND KIND LOVE LETTER.

STATE THE THINGS YOU'VE DONE WRONG (I.E. BEING HARSH CRITICAL, JUDGEMENTAL, MEAN, ETC.)

WRITE ABOUT THE IMPACT ON YOU (I.E. SELF-ESTEEM, MOTIVATION, ENERGY, ETC.)

LIST WHAT YOU PLAN TO DO DIFFERENTLY GOING FORWARD WHEN YOU "SLIP".

WRITE 3 THINGS YOU APPRECIATE ABOUT YOURSELF.

READ YOUR LOVE LETTER EACH NIGHT BEFORE BED.

Write it now.

Exercise #2: Mirror Work

Here's an exercise I would like you to practice that is going to help you hone in on this self-love. At some point, each and every day, you're going to be naked. When this moment comes, I want you to look at yourself in a full-length mirror—really look at yourself. Then I want you to adore, compliment, and give love to all the parts of you that normally don't receive so much love. Start to feel that vibration, the glow that radiates from self-love. Trust me, once you start loving yourself in this way, unconditionally, your entire world will be so much brighter. This is unconditional self-love in action.

Exercise #3: Review the Checklist Daily

Honestly complete the checklist each day, and never use it to shame yourself or feel bad about what didn't go well. THIS WILL NOT WORK. The purpose of the checklist is to celebrate your successes and to serve as a reminder to work on what didn't happen. Feel free to add your personal to-do's for wellbeing.

BEGIN A WILD AND UNCONDITIONAL LOVE AFFAIR WITH YOURSELF

ACTION	MON	TUE	WED	THR	FRI	SAT	SUN
GOT TO BED BETWEEN 9 PM - 11 PM.							
WOKE UP BETWEEN 6 AM - 8:30 AM							
MEDITATED (MINIMUM FIVE MINS).							
MOVED MY BODY (MINIMUM TEN MINS).							
SPENT INTENTIONAL TIME OUTDOORS (MINIMUM TEN MINS).							
ONE SUCCESS TODAY.							
ONE THING YOU ARE GRATEFUL FOR.							
PRACTICED SELF-LOVE TODAY.							
MAINTAINED HEALTHY BOUNDARIES (WORK, FRIENDS, PARTNER & FAMILY).							

ACTION	MON	TUE	WED	THR	FRI	SAT	SUN
ENJOYED A HEALTHY RELATIONSHIP WITH FOOD TODAY.							
ATE THREE TO FIVE SERVINGS OF VEGETABLES.							
DRANK PLENTY OF WATER.							
CONSUMED ENOUGH PROTEIN.							
ATE MINDFULLY.							
BRUSHED TEETH AFTER DINNER.							

WORDS TO LEAVE YOU WITH: YOU ARE ENOUGH

I never planned to help food addicts. Then one day, Daniela said to me, "Well, Sandra, I guess you are going to help food addicts."

"Food addicts?" I gasped. "Oh, no no no, I can't help food addicts. That is complicated. I wouldn't have anything to offer them."

Granted, I had lost 100 pounds and was a recovering food addict myself and had sponsored and mentored countless people to recovery. I figured that food addicts wanted skinny people to help them, like those on the covers of *Beauty* and *Shape* magazines.

I thought, *Don't you know that my biggest fear is that they will call me fat? And if they call me fat, I will crumble.*

"I can't," I concluded. "I just can't help food addicts."

"But what if you just tried?" She replied.

So I did. I put one tiny toe on the path. As soon as I set my foot down, the universe responded with a resounding YES. The opportunities, partnerships, and doctors came, and I was able to create Ontario's first outpatient program for food addicts. Then I helped create Canada's first residential treatment program. The programs were filling up. People were recovering. And the best part is, I was living my passion.

I took what I thought would be the greatest downfall of my life and turned it into a blessing because I get to serve each day.

Young me never thought I would be here today. The weight of my mother's struggles fell upon me, and every day was a fight to help make her better because if she was better, she could love me back. I was only five years old when I first remember seeing my mother have a nervous breakdown. I remember being so scared, not knowing what was happening or how to help.

At eight years of age, I became my mom's health-care advocate and translator. We were searching, searching, searching to make her better.

Tape Reel: The Question That Gives Me Purpose, JULY 1981

It is the summer between grades four and five. We are sitting in the doctor's office.

The doctor says, "Your mom will be dead in two months if she doesn't lose weight."

I look at my mom. I translate this into Italian in a way that allows her to understand what the doctor is saying without causing her to disintegrate into tears. I watch her sink into the chair and hold back her devastation. Here's a woman with four children, told to lose weight or die, and I had not even started grade five. A heavy shame settles upon my mom.

These scare tactics push her further into her depression and further into eating for comfort. Each time she seeks help, the finger of blame is pointed at her. It became clear what everyone thought: Don't ask for help because this is your fault. Time and time again, she is fat-shamed by doctors—the same doctors who take an oath to do no harm. Over the years, she suffers many more breakdowns and hospitalizations. Each and every time I fight tooth and nail to get her the help she needs. And every time, it seems like I am failing.

*From age four to thirty-four, my mother asks me the same question nearly every day: "Sandra, what have I done with my life?" It was a question too sophisticated for a five-year-old, but as an adult, I try to answer it every day in the work I do with others in Food Addiction Recovery. I now know through writing this book, that **the little girl inside of me is still trying to save my mother through all the food addicts I have the honor of working with.***

Today and every day, I dedicate my work to helping other food addicts in honor of my mom. My mom battled her addiction and mental health every day. I am sure she fought as hard as possible, but she never got the help she needed. Yet her strength and determination continue to inspire me, and I'm proud to carry on her legacy in my own way. I know that she would be proud of me, and I know that she is with me every step of the way. **Thank you, Mom, for everything. I love you.**

Often I speak to people interested in taking my Food Addiction Recovery program who are unsure whether they qualify as food addicts. I tell each person that whether you define yourself as a food addict or not, there is no downside to taking this program. We should all be eating whole, natural foods, regardless of whether we are living with elevated weight. Whether you are at your ideal weight or not, we should all be tapping into the divine magnificence and power within ourselves.

Whether you need to jump or just put your foot on the path, do it. By taking the first step, you can begin to get your life back on track. The journey may be difficult, but it is worth it. Surrounded by love and support, you can heal from food addiction and build a life that is joyous and fulfilling.

I Will Let You in on a Secret

This one is a big one. So lean in, take a deep breath, and let me show you the way.

Inside of me and you is this perfect place, a place of peace, where you fear nothing, where you lack nothing. This place inside of you is powerful. This place is magnificent. And your only job is to live from this place, create from this place, and see your value. When I live from this space, everything else falls into place. The people, the experiences, the opportunities—they all show up because I am aligned with my truth. And it starts with accessing this perfect place inside of you.

You **are enough** to carry this message with you and to others as you step into a world of possibility.

Remember my story of sitting under the willow tree? It was a moment of freedom, acceptance, and awakening. The time when I felt intense close-contact with my mother and God and heard the voice tell me, "You were never a food addict." That voice affirmed everything I believe about the healing power of spirituality—that we are all born with the spark of the Divine inside of us. I trust that if you follow the guidance laid out within the three pillars, you will have your own "under the willow tree" moment, and perhaps even many of them. Seek moments when you tap into your calm, confident, powerful center and know **you are enough** exactly as you are. Spirituality is remembering that and living from that place.

Every day, there are opportunities to catch a glimpse of your true nature and live from that place. It might be something as simple as taking a few deep breaths and feeling the ground beneath your feet. Or it might be watching the sunrise and remembering that you are part of something much larger. Whenever you take a moment to connect with your spirituality, you are reminded of your innate greatness, and you become more confident, peaceful, and powerful. By making spirituality part of your daily life, you can live from your center more often and make choices from a place of love and wisdom. As you do, you will see your life transform in ways you never imagined.

Let's Recap

This is the part of the book where I try my best to take everything and roll it all into key takeaways for you—a cheat sheet, if you will. It's the section where I say, "If you take anything away from this book, please let it be the following." Here we go.

1. Find peace with your body exactly as you are in this moment, knowing that **you are enough**.

   One of the greatest gifts you can give yourself is peace and neutrality with food. In Food Addiction Recovery, we often become so focused on food and our bodies that we forget to live. We forget to love ourselves and appreciate all that we are. But at this moment, **you are enough.** You are exactly as you should be. Take a deep breath and let go of all the negativity you have been carrying around. Forgive yourself for any mistakes you have made. Give yourself permission to love yourself exactly as you are in this moment. Then let go and move forward into the future with peace in your heart.

2. **You are enough** to overcome your cravings.

   We know by now that cravings can be incredibly powerful. The constant pull to eat certain foods, even when you're not hungry, can feel like an impossible force to resist. However, it's important to remember that cravings are nothing more than your body's response to certain triggers. They are neurological, biological, and hormonal in nature, and they do not control you. **You are enough** to overcome the waves of cravings.

   With each passing day, you are becoming stronger, more resilient, and more capable of making the food choices that are best for your body. So when a craving comes knocking, remind yourself that you have the power to say no. You control your food choices, and you are enough to overcome any obstacle.

3. Never enough is a LIE. Don't listen to the cunning lies that contain messages that you are never enough, said in countless ways, because **you are enough**.

    If you're like me, you've probably spent a lot of your life feeling like you're not good enough: not thin enough, not pretty enough, not smart enough—the list goes on. And it's all a lie.

    But here's the thing: **You ARE enough**. You are more than enough. In fact, you are perfect exactly the way you are.

    And I know that can be hard to believe, especially if you're caught up in the vicious cycle of food addiction. But it's true. You are worthy of love, happiness, and respect, no matter what your weight or waist size may be.

    So please, don't listen to the lies anymore. **You are Enough** with a capital "E."

4. Understand **you are enough,** and you will begin a wild, unconditional love affair with yourself.

    When I realized I was enough, it was like waking up from a food coma. For years, I'd been going on food binges and eating until I was physically ill, then shaming myself for days or even weeks at a time. But no matter how much I punished myself, I could never seem to lose the weight or get my eating under control. It wasn't until I realized **I am enough**—just as I am—that I finally started true healing. At that moment, I committed to ending my cycle of body hatred. And it was the best decision I ever made. Now, instead of using food to stuff down my feelings or numb out from my life, I use self-love and self-care to nurture myself. And as a result, my relationship with food and my body has radically transformed. I am finally free from the prison of food addiction and body loathing—and it all started with recognizing that **I am enough**.

    When you struggle with food addiction, it can feel like you will never be enough. You can beat yourself up for every mistake, every slip-up, and every moment of weakness. But the truth is, **you are enough**. **You are enough** to overcome food addiction and build a healthy, happy life.

5. **You are enough** to receive all the kind, loving and supportive energy from the Universe.

What you feed your mind is often more important than what you feed your body. When your mind is filled with negative thoughts and self-doubt, it is difficult to make positive changes in your life. But when you fill your mind with positive thoughts and self-love, change becomes possible.

Spirituality is the process of learning **you are enough** and therefore, having everything you need to recover from food addiction. By connecting with a higher power, you can find the strength and courage to continue on the path of healing. Tap into the power within you. You were born with the spark of the Divine inside of you. You were born with a magnificence—a calm, confident, powerful center. Nurture your spirituality and live from this place.

I'm so grateful to have found the Overeaters Anonymous program, though I'm no longer a member. I don't know where I would be without it. When I first came in, I was pretty resistant to the idea that a higher power would help me with my eating. I just couldn't wrap my head around it because I was angry at God. But the more I heard people share their stories, the more I realized maybe there was something to this after all. And the more I read *The Big Book of Alcoholics Anonymous*, the more sense it all started to make. I must have read this passage on page forty-five about twenty times before it sunk in. It explains, "The main object is to find a power greater than yourself." This is such an important concept for me because it does not say the mission is to merely stop using alcohol, or in my case food, but to tap into spirituality. Meaning, I am not expected to do this on my own, and I can rely on a higher power to help me through difficult times. This has been a great comfort to me, and I am so thankful for the wisdom contained in the *Big Book*. Now I can honestly say that I have surrendered to the magnificence within me, and since then, my life has never been better.

You Never Have to Diet, Ever Again

One day, I filmed a commercial for women's day. When it was time to film my part, the director pulled me aside for a few seconds before we started.

He said, "Sandra, I am so happy you are doing this work. I have worked with models for years and seen the extent of their restrictive diets. Sometimes they eat only a few almonds a day. Working with them is so difficult because, mentally, they are not present."

It was interesting to hear this, although it was something I had heard before. I realized that those models and I were not that different. The majority of their mental real estate was dedicated to how they can *not* eat. In contrast, mine focused on compulsive eating—how I *can* eat as often as possible. Both of us were fighting our compulsions around food.

After we were done filming, the director commended me on how few takes we shot. "Sandra, you're a star! You got it right the first time, and every time thereafter was the same."

"Thank you!" I smiled proudly.

You see, I am grateful that I didn't get what I wanted when I was the sickest—the cycle of restrictive dieting followed by binging. The years of yoyo dieting, thinking that a smaller dress size was the answer to my happiness and success, were draining. Every famine, which was every restrictive diet, was followed by a feast. This is because a restrictive diet sets off a cascade of events in the brain, totally outside your control, that make you seek food and eat food. You can't fight it. That is when the inner self-hatred begins: *Why couldn't I have just stuck it out?* This happened to me when I relapsed for over a year and a half and gained seventy pounds. I thought that if I could go back to that "plan," I could weigh 120 pounds. And if I saw the scale read 120, I would be happy. I would be enough. But it was never going to work. I thought I had failed, and I was never enough.

We blame ourselves for not sticking to a restrictive diet and losing the weight, but that was never possible. To top off this disappointment, our brains are fighting against us. All of these combined factors lead us to conclude how terrible we are.

I am grateful to walk the path of healing without diets or a scale, and this is the future I want to see, one where no one ever diets again, where we love and accept our bodies just as they are. I dream of a world where we view food as nourishment, not as something to fear or fight against. This starts with each individual making the decision to love and accept themselves just as they are—**enough.**

Look Through the Eyes of Love

A woman I worked with in a residential treatment center contacted me years later. She shared how our work together impacted her life:

"Sandra, I will never forget what you told me, and I still practice this every day. You told me to always look through the eyes of love. Look at myself through the eyes of love. Look at life through the eyes of love. Look at others through the eyes of love."

Hearing this warmed my heart. If you look through the eyes of love at yourself, the world, and the people around you, everything will work out. Why? Because inside of every one of us is the Divine. There is a God inside of us. If I ever feel discontent with a person, place, or situation, all I have to do is know that it is in the hands of their Divine power and my Divine power, and between them, everything will work out.

But it all starts with you. When you look at yourself through the eyes of love, you realize there is nothing wrong with you and there never was. You have been trying to fix something never wrong or broken. You just have to undo the stories, beliefs, and notions that you were never enough. Instead, look at yourself with kindness, love, and gratitude. Know that you are worthy of love and respect just as you are. Allow yourself to heal and move forward in your life with confidence and joy. It all starts with you: Believe in yourself and know that you are amazing just as you are!

I have a deep, deep love for my clients. I have grown to appreciate each one of them. I see the very best in them, which brings out the best in them. This love has allowed me to be there for them through the darkest of times and the most trying of obstacles. They are my light and my hope. Seeing them make progress—even small steps—fills me with immense satisfaction and joy. Knowing that I was able to help them get there is an indescribable feeling. It is my honor and privilege to serve them, and I will continue to do so with all of my heart.

The little girl inside of me who was not able to save her mother carries this into the work I do. I still hear my mom's voice in my head, *Sandra, what have I done with my life?*

That was her consistent question to me.

She meant it on two levels. First, she felt she had nothing to show for her life. And second, she had destroyed her life. It had a double-weighted meaning. Perhaps I am still that little girl trying to save my mom. All I know is that I want her life to have meaning. I hope through this book, I have given my mother—and so many others who lived in pain and suffering and passed away too soon—the compassionate meaning each and every one of their lives deserved.

APPENDIX

YOUR FOOD SERENITY JOURNEY

Chapter One Exercises

Exercise #1: Break Up with Your Scale

Examine your relationship with your scale. Is it neutral? Meaning, if you spent the last week eating on point and exercising, and your weight remains the same, or heaven forbid, you gain a pound—which, by the way, happens even when you do everything right—can you be neutral? Or does it make you want to throw in the towel?

It's always a red flag for me when a client adjusts her food intake to appease the scale. "How much can I eat without gaining weight? How much do I need to restrict to reach my goal-weight fast? I'm only going to eat this way so long as the scale keeps going down, but if it plateaus or dares go up a pound or two, I'm abandoning ship." These sentiments always make me sad. My client is completely missing the point. We eat whole, fresh foods because it feels amazing! Life feels different. We show up differently. We move our bodies every day because we are living organisms who need to exercise our flexibility, strength, and endurance to feel well. Stillness can potentially lead to illness.

You need and deserve a new measure of success. I always encourage my clients to measure non-scale victories to keep motivation high. Non-scale victories can include improved mood, energy, presence, and sleep; reduced need for medicines (with a doctor's approval); and regained ability to cross your legs or climb the stairs without experiencing pain or becoming winded. Become a detective for all

189

the ways you're improving. When you can see you're winning, you'll want to keep going. Nothing slows you down more than discouragement.

I want you to consider whether your relationship with the scale is abusive:

1. Does the scale determine if it is going to be a good day or a bad day?
2. Does it dictate whether you are a good or bad person?
3. Does the number on the scale tell you what you should or shouldn't eat that day?
4. Is the scale your only measure of success?

If you answered yes to most of these questions, your relationship with the scale is toxic. It's time to cut ties and break up.

I get why your doctor, surgeon, and maybe even your pharmacist or dentist need to know what you weigh. But why do you need to know? If you're doing your best, eating whole foods, and moving your body, why does it matter what you weigh? Isn't your real job to love the body you have?

Take a few moments now to journal about the above questions:

_____

_____

_____

_____

_____

_____

Exercise #2: Identify Your Patterns

At what point did eating and your weight begin to feel like a problem in your life. This exercise will help you see patterns in your eating habits. Ask yourself:

1. What falsehoods did you believe about food or your body?
2. What messages did you hear, accept, and repeat about food or your body?
3. Which of these beliefs do you now need to let go of?

	BELIEFS ABOUT EATING FOOD	BELIEFS ABOUT YOUR WEIGHT	DO YOU STILL BELIEVE THIS? YES OR NO
0 - 5 YEARS OF AGE			
6 - 9 YEARS OF AGE			
10 - 12 YEARS OF AGE			
13 - 19 YEARS OF AGE			
20 - 29 YEARS OF AGE			
30 - 39 YEARS OF AGE			
40 + YEARS OF AGE			

Chapter Two Exercises

Exercise #1: In What State Are You Eating?

I've never been a fan of food journaling, the act is always so triggering for me. I was happy to record everything I ate when I was "perfect." However, when I compulsively overate, it felt too humiliating to record what I was eating, much less share it with another person.

In this journal, don't be too concerned about the food, though it will offer clues to your eating triggers. This exercise is more about discovering your personal patterns of eating that are both helpful and unhelpful.

As you consistently collect data on when you eat, why you eat, and what you eat, you will begin to understand what drives you to eat. You will gain the most valuable information when you record meals that have not gone according to plan. Drop the judgment if you want to find true answers and solutions.

When recording the times at which you eat, pay attention to the number of hours between meals and how that affects your hunger level at each meal and the food choices you make. When recording your Emotional State prior to a meal, begin noticing themes among circumstances that lead you to consume food for comfort or escape. When recording your Emotional State after a meal, try to recognize trends that may help you better understand your relationship with food.

Example:

TIME	8AM	1PM	6PM	8PM
MEAL	BREAKFAST	LUNCH	DINNER	SNACK
EMOTIONAL STATE BEFORE MEAL NEUTRAL, CONTENT, BORED, LONELY, SAD, GUILTY, STRESSED, ANGRY...				
HUNGER LEVEL (1-5) BEFORE MEAL 1- RAVENOUS 2- REASONABLE 3-NEUTRAL 4- COMFORTABLE 5- FULL TO THE POINT OF FEELING ILL				
FOOD(S) EATEN				
HUNGER LEVEL (1-5) AFTER MEAL				
EMOTIONAL STATE AFTER MEAL NEUTRAL, CONTENT, BORED, LONELY, SAD, GUILTY, STRESSED, ANGRY...				

Chapter Three Exercises

Exercise #1: Identify Your Trigger Foods

Write down your addictive foods or trigger foods. These are foods that you obsess about. Once you start eating a trigger food, it is very difficult to stop or have a reasonable portion. Eating your trigger foods often leads to an overeating episode containing other foods. These foods almost always contain refined sugar and refined flour.

Ask yourself:

- What do I eat when I experience strong emotions? (i.e., anger, sadness, stress, excitement, happiness.)
- What is the personal price I've paid for continuing to eat addictive foods?
- What price have I paid physically, emotionally, and spiritually?
- What have trigger foods robbed me of?
- What opportunities have I lost?
- What are my behaviors that lead to overeating? (i.e., eating in front of a screen, eating in the car, eating standing up at the kitchen counter.)

Hint: You can keep it simple. You may notice that all your trigger foods contain refined sugar and refined flour, or have been deep fried. Please keep in mind, some trigger foods don't have sugar or flour (i.e., chips, which is one of the most addictive foods on the planet). Make sure to list those foods as well.

Exercise #2: Identify Your Lies

What are the top five lies your addict voice uses when you have a craving? Examples below:

- Have one bite—you can handle it.
- Don't worry, you will start the diet tomorrow.
- It's too hard to eat right today. You are too stressed, too sad, and nothing is going your way.
- You deserve a treat.

....

....

....

....

....

....

....

....

....

Exercise #3: Manage Your Cravings

Refer to the three-step CBT (Cognitive Behavior Therapy) technique when you need it. I suggest taking a picture of the technique or printing it so you can easily focus on the steps in a high-risk situation and effectively manage your cravings.

ALL CRAVINGS ARE LIES.

A CRAVING COULD BE SEEN AS A BRAIN GLITCH.

A CRAVING CAN BE ANXIETY INDUCING.

TAKE 10 DEEP GROUNDING BREATHS.

Chapter Four Exercises.

Exercise #1: Create Your Own Mantra

Retrain your brain. Give your subconscious mind instructions for creating the body, health, and life of your dreams. Take a moment to write a mantra for yourself. It should be simple and positive. Here are some examples:

"I look at life through the eyes of love. I can see all that is right and beautiful about me."

"I was born with the spark of the Divine. This flame of magnificence burns bright inside of me."

"I invite the Divine to guide my thinking, my actions, and my words today."

"My life is filled with blessings and miracles."

_____

_____

_____

_____

_____

_____

Say this mantra with intensity and often! Every time you get up to go to the washroom, walk to your car, or pour a glass of water, press play on your mantra.

Exercise #2: Reframe Your Monologue After a Slip with Food

Think back to your last compulsive eating episode. What was happening at the time? Can you imagine showing yourself compassionate curiosity during that time? Were you calling for love? Journal here about your call for love:

_____

_____

_____

_____

_____

_____

Exercise #3: Begin the Journey to Meditation

There is no wrong way to meditate. You will never master meditation, and every session is a chance to know yourself better. You are a physical, mental, and spiritual being. Each of these areas needs time, attention, and care. Take time to research three different approaches or practices to meditation. Record your research findings here:

Chapter Five Exercises

Exercise #1: Believe in Miracles

You are the architect of your life. Every structure begins with a thought. Then the architect takes pen to paper to draw out her idea. No one stands behind the architect and says, "There's no building there—it's just a pile of dirt." Our new life begins with a thought, a thought brought to life on paper, a belief that this new life is possible.

It starts with a thought.
It's designed on paper with great detail.
Then, it comes into manifestation.

I want you, if just for a moment, to believe that a miracle has occurred. The miracle is that your problems with food are gone, and you have healthy, beautiful relationships with your body, with God, and with food.

Define your Higher Power:

_____

_____

_____

_____

What does this Higher Power want for you?

_____

_____

_____

What do you want from this Higher Power?

_____

_____

_____

Describe the relationship you want with food?

_____

_____

_____

_____

Exercise #2: Build Your Village of Support

My village started in the rooms of Overeaters Anonymous, where I took my first baby steps towards food serenity. I stopped weighing myself and instead focused on developing a healthy relationship with food and myself. I learned about the importance of getting proper sleep, developed a sustainable meal plan, and started exercising regularly.

Take a look at the village of support below. I want you to give each element a score out of 10. A score of 0/10 means you are struggling with that aspect of your health, and a score of 10/10 means you have mastered the element.

List the areas of your life that received low scores and outline your plan to address them and build your village of support:

_____

_____

_____

_____

_____

Chapter Six Exercises

Exercise #1: Strike a Balance Between Your Values and Self-Love

DEFINE YOUR NEEDS AND PLAN OF SELF CARE

DETERMINE WHAT YOU ARE WILLING TO GIVE

PRIORITIZE OVER THE NEEDS OF OTHERS.

AND THEN STOP-- NO MATTER WHAT.

The purpose of this exercise is to determine how to balance your self-love and self-care with helping others. When doing this exercise, I want you to consider someone in your life with whom you struggle to maintain boundaries, someone who often leaves you depleted.

First thing's first—define what your needs are. Start with the basics: sleep, healthy meals, time spent outdoors, meditation, and movement.

Step #1: List your needs to be well:

....

....

....

....

....

In a codependent relationship, both individuals tend to overlook their own needs in order to please the other person. As a result, each person ends up feeling drained and resentful. If you find yourself in a codependent relationship, it is important to take a step back and assess your needs. What are you sacrificing in order to keep the other person happy? Is it your time, your interests, or your dreams? Once you have identified your needs, you can start taking the steps necessary to fulfill them. This may mean setting aside time for yourself, pursuing your own interests, or communicating your needs. It is also important to remember that you cannot make the other person happy; only they can do that. By taking care of yourself and setting boundaries, you can begin to build a healthier, more balanced relationship.

Step #2: What am I willing to give?
Identify a person or institution (i.e. work, church, etc.) with which you may be codependent.

_____

Now consider how much time and energy you have left to give after all your needs are met. What can you comfortably give in terms of time, energy, and sometimes even finances. You may also find that it's better not to give in this situation, and that's okay.

Time
_____

_____

_____

Energy
_____

_____

_____

Finances

....

....

....

This is your quota for helping this person or institution. Once you've reached your quota for the week, month, or year (whatever you set out), then it is time to release this person or institution to find their own way. Otherwise, you may be robbing them of the opportunity to grow stronger. This is not an easy road, but it is often the road to freedom for you both.

Chapter Seven Exercises

Exercise #1: A Life in Review

- Are you in a relationship that nurtures your spirit and enhances your life?
- Does your career inspire you?
- Do you have the necessary boundaries in place to live a healthy, whole life?
- Do you care for and nourish your body, mind, and spirit?
- Are the thoughts that occupy your mind energizing?

To survive a dysfunctional lifestyle, we must lie to ourselves to make the chaos bearable. What lies are you telling yourself about the broken areas of your life?

....

....

....

....

....

....

Exercise #2: Proud of Myself

This next exercise is very powerful if you suffer with low self-worth. Each night before you fall asleep, I want you to review your day and pick one action that you are proud of. Next, and this is the most important piece, identify what this action means about you and who you are becoming.

For example, if you completed the exercises in this chapter, you can record that accomplishment as something you are proud of. When answering what this means about you, you can list qualities like those found below:

- Committed to getting better
- A hard worker
- Open
- Seeing possibilities

I AM PROUD OF MYSELF TODAY FOR:

....

....

....

....

....

....

THIS MEANS I AM:

✓	SMART	✓	CAPABLE
✓	CARING	✓	STRONG
✓	FUNNY	✓	CREATIVE
✓	LOVING	✓	BRAVE

...AND SO MUCH MORE!

Chapter Eight Exercises

Exercise #1: Uncovering Your Truths

I've shared with you my why, my growth, and my tribulations. Now it's your turn to uncover your truths. What is your why? What is your inspiration? What's going to keep you going?

_____

_____

_____

_____

Pillar #1: Eliminate Trigger Foods

- What is your defined meal plan?
- What are your red light foods and green light foods?
- Will you weigh and measure yourself?

Pillar #2: Develop Spirituality and Mindfulness

- What is your spiritual practice?
- What does it entail?
- How much time will you give to this each day?
- What time of day will this happen?

Pillar #3: Belong to a Support Network

- What is your support group?
- When do they meet?
- Where do they meet?
- Do you want a sponsor/mentor?
- Do you need professional help?

Based on the three pillars, create your plan of recovery.

Step #1: Identify and cut out your trigger foods:

....

....

....

....

Step #2: Design a spirituality practice (where, when, and how will you be mindful?):

....

....

....

....

Step #3: Develop a support system of people who understand your recovery and will encourage you on the path to food serenity:

_____

_____

_____

Chapter Nine Exercises

Exercise #1: Forgiveness

It is time to forgive yourself and to do so in a letter to yourself.

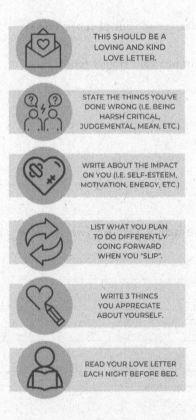

THIS SHOULD BE A LOVING AND KIND LOVE LETTER.

STATE THE THINGS YOU'VE DONE WRONG (I.E. BEING HARSH CRITICAL, JUDGEMENTAL, MEAN, ETC.)

WRITE ABOUT THE IMPACT ON YOU (I.E. SELF-ESTEEM, MOTIVATION, ENERGY, ETC.)

LIST WHAT YOU PLAN TO DO DIFFERENTLY GOING FORWARD WHEN YOU "SLIP".

WRITE 3 THINGS YOU APPRECIATE ABOUT YOURSELF.

READ YOUR LOVE LETTER EACH NIGHT BEFORE BED.

Write it now.

_____

_____

_____

_____

_____

_____

_____

_____

_____

_____

_____

_____

_____

_____

_____

_____

Exercise #2: Mirror Work

Here's an exercise I would like you to practice that is going to help you hone in on this self-love. At some point, each and every day, you're going to be naked. When this moment comes, I want you to look at yourself in a full-length mirror—really look at yourself. Then I want you to adore, compliment, and give love to all the parts of you that normally don't receive so much love. Start to feel that vibration, the glow that radiates from self-love. Trust me, once you start loving yourself in this way, unconditionally, your entire world will be so much brighter. This is unconditional self-love in action.

Exercise #3: Review the Checklist Daily

Honestly complete the checklist each day, and never use it to shame yourself or feel bad about what didn't go well. THIS WILL NOT WORK. The purpose of the checklist is to celebrate your successes and to serve as a reminder to work on what didn't happen. Feel free to add your personal to-do's for wellbeing.

ACTION	MON	TUE	WED	THR	FRI	SAT	SUN
GOT TO BED BETWEEN 9 PM - 11 PM.							
WOKE UP BETWEEN 6 AM - 8:30 AM							
MEDITATED (MINIMUM FIVE MINS).							
MOVED MY BODY (MINIMUM TEN MINS).							
SPENT INTENTIONAL TIME OUTDOORS (MINIMUM TEN MINS).							
ONE SUCCESS TODAY.							
ONE THING YOU ARE GRATEFUL FOR.							
PRACTICED SELF-LOVE TODAY.							
MAINTAINED HEALTHY BOUNDARIES (WORK, FRIENDS, PARTNER & FAMILY).							

ACTION	MON	TUE	WED	THR	FRI	SAT	SUN
ENJOYED A HEALTHY RELATIONSHIP WITH FOOD TODAY.							
ATE THREE TO FIVE SERVINGS OF VEGETABLES.							
DRANK PLENTY OF WATER.							
CONSUMED ENOUGH PROTEIN.							
ATE MINDFULLY.							
BRUSHED TEETH AFTER DINNER.							

ABOUT THE AUTHOR

As one of the world's first Certified Food Addiction Counselors, Sandra Elia is a true pioneer in the field of recovery from compulsive and addictive eating. Her expertise has brought about partnerships with Canada's top obesity and addiction doctors. Her Food Addiction Recovery Program invites clients to radically reconsider their understanding of food and its relationship to physical, emotional, and spiritual wellbeing.

Sandra runs her outpatient Food Addiction Recovery Program in clinics across Canada. She co-created Canada's first twenty-eight-day inpatient treatment program for food addiction at an addiction rehab centre in Toronto. Her programs dive deep into the unique and shared nature of our complicated relationships with food.

Sandra Elia knows firsthand the struggle of living with obesity. She has lived two lives: one as a woman living with obesity for fifteen years. She experienced a world that was not made for her size, seeking assistance from biased healthcare providers and dealing with fat-shaming. Since those difficult days, Sandra has transformed her life, developing a peaceful and healthy relationship with food.

Sandra is dedicated to changing the conversation so that anyone living with food addiction has access to treatment that is rooted in dignity, respect, and understanding.

Sandra's most important role to date is being a single mom to her beautiful daughter Sofia, doing her best to model a life that prioritizes happiness, health, and self-love. Sandra finds joy by dancing at any chance she gets and is a risk-taker on stage, relishing at any opportunity for competitive motivational speaking (several talks have gone viral!). She remains grounded by a spiritual practice that has been nurtured for over 20 years.

Sandra's work has been featured on The National Post, Global News Toronto, Global News Edmonton, CTV News Atlantic, Toronto Star, Toronto Sun, and radio shows across North America.

Website: *www.sandraelia.com*
Facebook: *@FoodAddictionProgram*
Instagram: *@sandraelia.ca*
LinkedIn: *@Sandra-Elia*

Printed in the USA
CPSIA information can be obtained
at www.ICGtesting.com
LVHW031804050624
782389LV00006B/489

9 781990 700187